D0604138

Jonathan Fong's
Walls that Wow

Jonathan Fong's
Walls that Wow

CREATIVE WALL TREATMENTS
without FANCY-SCHMANCY PAINTING

PHOTOGRAPHY BY Jessica Boone

WATSON-GUPTILL PUBLICATIONS / NEW YORK

First published in 2005 by Watson-Guptill Publications, a division of
VNU Business Media, Inc., 770 Broadway, New York, NY 10003
www.wgpub.com

Library of Congress Control Number: 2005925435
ISBN: 0-8230-6981-8

Senior Acquisitions Editor: Victoria Craven
Editor: Holly Jennings
Designer: Pooja Bakri Design
Production Manager: Ellen Greene

Printed in England

First printing 2005

1 2 3 4 5 6 7 8 9/13 12 11 10 09 08 07 06 05

Text set in FF Scala and Today SB

For Mom,
which is actually "Wow"
spelled upside down

Contents

Foreword

Jonathan Fong is my kind of guy. He thinks outside the box. He's enthusiastic. Passionate. Clever. He's not formally trained, and yet he's unbelievably creative. And he comes up with uniquely clever concepts with items that are available and affordable.

I met Jonathan when he was a guest on my HGTV show, *Kitty Bartholomew: You're Home.* For the show, I visited him at his townhouse in Santa Monica. He was so nervous to be on television for the first time, but he had nothing to worry about. For his regular job, he worked for an advertising agency, but it was obvious to me that his talent went way beyond catchy slogans. On my show, I thought I'd seen everything, but Jonathan was an original. He did truly amazing things to his own place. I could see right away that he was outrageously talented at putting things together that you would never have imagined. The things he was doing to his walls were fantastic. I was in awe. Because he didn't have all this training, he didn't even know he was "breaking the rules." This is why I say, "Ignorance is bliss." He has pure inspiration.

So I encouraged Jonathan to make a left turn. I kept saying, "You have a career in design." He said, "Really? Do you think so?" So I gave him an assignment. I told him that his kitchen was really boring and that he had to do something with it. A while later, he called me and told me I had to see his kitchen. Again, I was blown away. There was no other kitchen in the world like it. I don't think he copies anybody. He solves his own decorating problems in totally unique ways. And he literally gets his hands dirty and does the things he comes up with. I'd call it applied arts. He does stuff with everyday materials and creates magic.

So now that Jonathan has his own book series coming out, has it gone to his head? Not at all! He's not even a little bit uppity. He's very humble, and so grateful, and that's refreshing. Of all the people I've helped with their careers, he's the most grateful. For me, it was lucky happenstance that our paths met.

Sometimes what we need is a pat on the back and someone to say, "You can do it." I knew Jonathan could do it, and he has. I once told him it was now his responsibility to help someone else. And I'm happy to say he carries that attitude into this book. He cares. And his "anybody can do it" philosophy is contagious.

What fun it will be to watch where Jonathan goes from here. The sky's the limit for him. If I were to buy stock in the future, I'd buy stock in him. Like I said, he's my kind of guy.

Kitty Bartholomew
TV Host of *Kitty Bartholomew: You're Home*, HGTV

Introduction

Artistically challenged home decorators unite!

Can't draw? Neither can I. Can't paint? Ditto. When I began decorating my own home, wondering how to adorn the walls, I thought I'd try faux finishing. I was seeing it everywhere in magazines and books, and I liked the idea. Hey, I can do that! Yeah, right. As I learned about techniques like color washing, ragging, and stippling, I became discouraged. Faux finishing required patience and artistic ability, neither of which I had. I didn't care how easy the books said it was. One wrong move with my paintbrush and my wall would be ruined.

That's when I began creating my own wall treatments, ones that were visually spectacular, but didn't demand complicated painting techniques. My wall treatments used unexpected materials like fabric, metal, and cardboard, and required only simple tasks like cutting and stapling. Tasks that any beginner, like myself, could do—by myself!

If you've been intimidated by faux finishing, have great taste but horrible artistic skills, or are looking for original, inspirational ideas, then this book is for you. In the following pages, you'll find twenty-four stunning wall treatments with step-by-step instructions that are actually easy to follow. Normal people without degrees in art or interior design have successfully followed these same instructions and kept their sanity and self-respect. As an added bonus, many of these wall treatments are ideal for apartment renters or students in dormitories, who aren't allowed to paint or put anything permanent on their walls.

I've even recommended some music to listen to while creating each wall, to put you in the right mood.

For each wall, I've indicated the approximate time it will take to complete the project, as well as the "Level of Ease," ranging from 1 to 5, with 1 being easiest. There's no "level of difficulty" here.

LEVEL OF EASE

1. It doesn't get any easier than this.
2. Easy as pie (a heat-and-serve pie).
3. So easy, you'll feel like you deserve your own decorating show.
4. A lot easier than you thought it would be.
5. Easy—if you follow my directions.

Before starting a project, be sure to read all the instructions from start to finish, so you have a general idea of the process. Most projects require basic tools that you probably already have around the house—like scissors, a hammer, an X-Acto®, a straightedge, and a tape measure. Each chapter begins with a list of everything you'll need to complete the wall treatment—from the most basic tools to additional, harder-to-find materials. And don't worry, I'll tell you where to buy everything (except I figure you know where to find a packet of nails). If you have questions or comments, I'd love to hear from you. You can e-mail me through my Web site: jonathanfongstyle.com. And please send me photos of the wall projects you complete; that would simply make my day.

Whether you live in a traditional Cape Cod or an urban loft, you will find wall ideas that fit your personal style. So forge ahead with confidence. You might not be able to paint (or even pronounce) *trompe l'oeil*. But with this book you will be creating something even better—Walls that Wow.

Part I:
Fabric-adabra

If you think paint gives you options, wait till you try fabric. Fabric goes beyond just color, adding the extra dimension of pattern and texture. The result is a richness that has to be seen—and felt—to be believed. Try velvets and silk brocades for a luxurious feel. Perhaps jacquards, florals, and stripes for the French country look. Or even denim and corduroy for a Western motif. Just step into a fabric store, and you'll be filled with ideas and inspiration.

Chapter 1

Penthouse View: A Dramatic Patchwork of Satins and Furs

LEVEL OF EASE: 4

ETW (ESTIMATED TIME OF WOW): 15 minutes per panel

RECOMMENDED MUSIC: Carole King. *Tapestry*

When I first demonstrated this fabric wall treatment on the Home and Garden Television (HGTV) network, I was surprised by the tremendous response it got from viewers. The wall really struck a chord with home crafters looking for a stylish decorating solution that didn't require painting. It's so easy. First, fabric is wrapped around individual foam core panels. Then the panels are applied to the wall with Velcro™. You can even remove the panels at any time to be cleaned or replaced.

This particular project allows you to mix and match up to four complementary fabrics to create a dramatic patchwork. Pictured to the left is a luxurious combination of satins, quilting, and faux fur that would make Jean Harlow feel right at home. I originally created this wall for my bedroom. I wanted to design an all-white room but was afraid that all-white would be a bit sterile. Then, as I was browsing through a friend's wedding magazine, I fell in love with the fabrics associated with weddings and came upon the idea that I could make white more interesting by varying the textures, as well as by playing with its various shades. The rest is history. Let me tell you, every time I walk into my bedroom I feel like I'm staying in a luxurious hotel. The only problem is that this wall treatment does not magically come with room service.

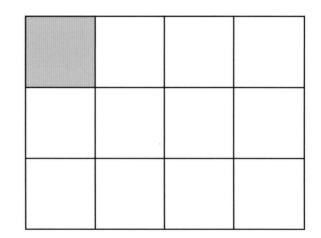

1 MEASURE THE PANELS

First, you'll want to decide how large you want your panels to be. Do you want the effect of a few big panels on your wall or a lot of small ones? (Take it from me, the larger—and fewer—panels you have, the less work you'll have to do.) Draw a diagram of the dimensions of your wall and then divide that space into a grid. A four-across, three-down grid, like the one in the diagram here, works well. Because most walls are 8 feet high, three panels running vertically will work perfectly for most rooms. How many panels you have going horizontally will depend on how wide your wall is.

To determine the measurements of each panel, divide the wall dimensions by the number of panels you'd like. Say your wall is 96 inches high. If you wanted three panels down, just divide 96 inches by three, and each panel will be 32 inches high. Do the same for the width of the wall. To give you some visual reference, the dimensions of the panels shown on pages 14–15 are 32 x 32 inches.

WHERE TO BUY IT

The foundation of each panel is a very lightweight material called foam core. This wonderful invention comes in standard-sized boards of 32 x 40 inches. You can buy them at any art supply store for about $5 a board. They come in black or white. For the wall treatment in this chapter, I used the black foam core so the fabric and Velcro would stand out, but I actually prefer the white foam core. It has a semiglossy outer layer that is more durable than the black foam core's matte finish. As for the fabric, stop by your neighborhood fabric store and see what they have. Be on the lookout for closeouts and clearance fabrics, since you don't need a lot of yardage for this project. I love stepping into a fabric store, because it's full of possibilities. Nestled next to the hideous prints that remind me of blouses my mother wore in the 1970s, I always find some unique color or texture that inspires me. But be careful. Buying fabric can be addictive. I have piles of remnants in my office as proof.

2 CUT THE FOAM CORE TO SIZE

Using an X-Acto knife and a straightedge, cut your foam core to the size you want your panels to be. You will be adding padding and fabric to the foam core, so you have to compensate by about a half-inch for the added thickness when sizing it. To illustrate, if you want a panel that's 32 inches wide, then you should cut the foam core to 31-1/2 inches to allow for the added padding and fabric.

HELPFUL HINT

Be very careful with your X-Acto knife. Cut gently and slowly, and be sure to change your blade frequently so it glides smoothly. Remember, even though it's easy to cut foam core, it's also easy to veer offtrack and cut yourself. I actually use an oven mitt on the hand that's holding the straightedge. It's goofy, but at least I still have all my fingers. Also, use a cutting mat, or even a large piece of cardboard, underneath the foam core to protect your floors, tabletop, or whatever surface you're cutting on.

3 CUT THE PADDING AND FABRIC

Padding gives each panel depth, as well as that soft, cushy look and feel. It also helps when you align the panels side by side, hiding your not-so-straight edges. For padding, use polyester batting that you can find at any fabric or upholstery store. (For heavier fabrics like faux fur, you actually don't need padding because it's already so thick.) Trim the batting for each panel so that it's about an inch wider on every side than the foam core. The photograph shows how easy it is to cut the padding to the correct size by using the foam core as a guide.

Now take your fabric and cut it so that it's about an inch wider on every side than the batting. If the foam core is 32 x 30 inches and the batting is 34 x 32, then the fabric should be trimmed to about 36 x 34. Remember, you don't have to be perfect, or even close to perfect. Just eyeball it.

CLOSE ENOUGH

You may be thinking here, "What if I don't get the dimensions exactly right? What if I'm off by an inch?" Don't worry about it. To the naked eye, any mistakes won't be detectable; and if they are, people will think it's supposed to be that way. From a practical standpoint, the padding and fabric you add are squeezable and expandable, so they will compensate for any irregularities in the foam core sizing.

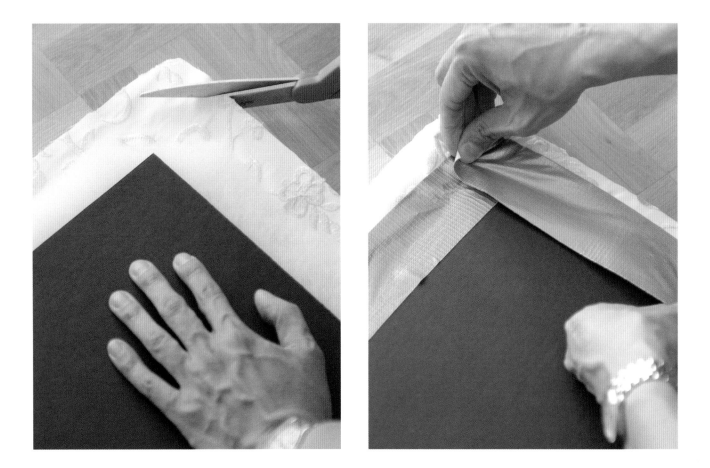

4 WRAP THE PADDING AND FABRIC AROUND THE FOAM CORE

Place the trimmed fabric upside down on your work surface. On top of the fabric, center your batting. And on top of the batting, center your foam core. As shown in the photograph (above, left), trim the corners of the batting at a 45-degree angle to the corners of the foam core. This will eliminate extra bulk in the corners when you fold the batting over. Then trim the corners of the fabric so they are about an inch wider than where the batting is trimmed.

Working one edge at a time, wrap the batting and fabric around the foam core and secure it in place with duct tape. When all four sides are secured, you may want to add extra tape at the corners to help secure them. I like duct tape because it holds well but is also forgiving, so you can adjust it on the foam core if you need to. For heavier or more textured fabrics like faux fur, duct tape doesn't work as well. That's when you use a staple gun. And don't worry if the back of your panel looks like a mess. No one will see it.

KEEPING IT CLEAN

These fabric panels might look like a cleaning nightmare, but maintenance is actually quite simple. Because the panels are attached with Velcro, just remove them from the wall and vacuum them, using the upholstery attachment of your vacuum cleaner. If the extension hose on your vacuum cleaner is long enough, you don't even need to remove the panels.

5 ATTACH THE PANEL TO THE WALL

To attach the panels to the wall, use Velcro rather than nails or double-sided tape. Velcro allows you to reposition the panels if you need to, and we're all about being forgiving. Velcro comes in different grades. Don't use the inexpensive craft Velcro. Select the industrial grade rolls sold in hardware stores. People often ask me if Velcro will take the paint off their walls. I've never had a problem, but it depends on your wall and paint type. Experiment on a hidden corner of the wall if you're concerned.

Cut squares of the "fuzzy" portion of the Velcro and stick them to the four corners of the foam core that are not covered with duct tape. Now comes the nifty part. Instead of sticking the "spiky" portion of the Velcro on the wall and praying that the fuzzy and spiky sections match up, cut squares of the spiky portion and place them face down right on the fuzzy part that's already on the panel. Then take the protective backing off the spiky portion, as shown in the photograph above, and attach the whole panel to the wall. Press the panel firmly on the wall where the Velcro is, so the adhesive attaches. Repeat this process for all the panels, and you're done. Wasn't that easy?

Chapter 2

Don't Rain on My Brocade: A Quick and Easy Makeover with Fabric

LEVEL OF EASE: ③

ETW (ESTIMATED TIME OF WOW): 4 hours

RECOMMENDED MUSIC: *Amelie* soundtrack

The fabric panels in the last chapter are a great way to apply fabric to a wall. They allow you to use more than one fabric, and the portability of the panels is a big advantage. However, if you want to use the same fabric throughout the room, or you don't have the time to wrap individual panels, there is an easier method. And that would be stapling.

Stapling fabric directly on the wall is a cinch. In fact, I installed this brocade fabric on all four walls by myself in about four hours. This wall was part of a weekend makeover surprise in which I transformed a plain, white bedroom into a red, French-vintage boudoir. I had very little time to do the transformation, and unlike those television makeover shows, I didn't have an entire crew to help me. I was on my own. The stapling method got the job done. And fabulously, if I do say so myself.

Of course, you don't have to use brocade for this project. I've always thought walls of wet vinyl would be spectacular, and linen is always a tasteful alternative. Because you're covering an entire wall with one fabric, you have to think what would look good on a large scale, and what would match the furniture and accessories you are planning to use. To be honest, I'm not a brocade kind of guy. But the design matched the look I was going for.

WHAT YOU'LL NEED

Fabric by the yard
Glue sticks for hot-glue gun
Hammer
Hot-glue gun
Pushpins
Ribbon trim
Staple gun
3M® Super 77® Spray
  Adhesive

WHERE TO BUY IT

I've already talked about exploring your local fabric store in the last chapter. That's also where you'll find ribbon trim for this project. As for the other supplies, buy your staple gun at the hardware store. And if you don't already have a hot-glue gun, run over to an arts and crafts store to get one. They're extremely fun. I recommend the cordless kind, because the ones you plug in have impossibly short cords. The arts and crafts store is also the place to buy spray adhesive.

1 DETERMINE HOW MUCH FABRIC TO PURCHASE

Because a typical wall is 8 feet high, you'll need a length of 3 yards (9 feet) of fabric to run from the top of the wall to the bottom. Now, how many of these 3-yard lengths will you need? A standard bolt of fabric is 54 inches wide, so divide the width of your wall in 54-inch increments. For example, if your wall is 144 inches (12 feet) wide, divide 144 by 54 and you'll get 2.67, or 3, since you'll want to round up. Therefore, you'll need three 3-yard lengths, or 9 yards of fabric altogether.

If you have windows and doors on your wall, you will need less fabric, but I recommend that you purchase more fabric anyway. It's good to have extra on hand if you make a mistake. And the extra fabric is great for making throw pillows (as if I could sew).

2 CREATE A HEM FOR THE FABRIC

First, cut your fabric so it's slightly longer than the height of your wall. Then hold up a piece of your fabric at the far left side of the wall and fold the top edge down on the underside to create a hem of about 2 inches. Stretch the fabric taut so there is no slack. If your fabric has a pattern, you can use your pattern to help you line up the hem. For example, I made sure the curlicues in this brocade lined up at the top.

AN OPTIONAL STEP

Before attaching the fabric, you can staple 1-inch-thick polyester batting to the wall. Most walls are not perfectly straight and the batting helps the fabric lay flat. Without it, the fabric can billow out. But since I was in a hurry for this weekend makeover, I ignored this step. If you, too, skip the batting, just be sure to stretch the fabric out on the wall as straight as possible, since you won't have the batting to hide the flaws.

3 STAPLE THE FIRST LENGTH OF FABRIC

Keep folding the hem down as you staple across the top of the fabric. Although I did this myself, it helps to have someone hold one end of the fabric for you. If you're going it alone, the trick is to use a pushpin to hold one end of the fabric while stapling the other.

After you've stapled the top of the fabric, you can proceed to the sides. Stretch the fabric so it lies smooth across the wall and, again, fold the fabric under to create a hem at the sides.

Staple the sides every few feet with the staples running vertically. Finally, staple the bottom of the fabric, folding it to create a hem at the bottom as well. If you have an electrical outlet at the bottom of the wall, cut a hole in the fabric around the outlet and staple the edges.

If your wall is made of plaster or the drywall is particularly tough, the staples may not penetrate all the way. If that happens, just tap the staples with a hammer till they're completely in the wall.

HELPFUL HINT

There are manual staple guns and there are electric ones. I would recommend an electric one. I used a manual staple gun for this wall, and by the time I was finished, my poor little hand was paralyzed and frozen in the stapling position. Not pretty.

4 ATTACH THE ADJACENT PIECES

On to the next piece of fabric. When stapling fabric that's adjacent to another piece, try to line up the pieces so that the pattern is continuous. After stapling the top to hold the fabric in place, you can staple the sides. Again, fold down the side to create a hem, stretch it tight, and staple vertically. There will be a small seam, but that's okay. You will be covering it up later with some trim.

5 HIDE THE STAPLES

If your fabric is dark, you will hardly see the staples. Still, it's always a good idea to hide them to give the wall a finished look. Also, you want to hide the seam created by two adjacent pieces of fabric. Find some ribbon trim that coordinates with your fabric and cut it to size. Put a thin line of hot glue on one side of the trim and glue the piece on the seam. Be careful when pressing down on the trim because the hot glue can burn your fingers.

6 AN OPTIONAL BORDER

This particular wall had a curved ceiling, so there was no definitive point where the wall ended and the ceiling began. Therefore, I created one. I found old sheet music and applied 3M Super 77 Spray Adhesive to the backs of the sheets and then adhered them to the wall above the fabric. (When using a spray adhesive, I recommend using it outside and placing a large piece of cardboard or old newspapers under whatever you're spraying.) The row of sheet music formed a straight line that acted as the top of the wall. Then I stapled a tassel trim at the top to accentuate the line.

KEEPING IT CLEAN

As with the fabric panels in the previous chapter, vacuuming with a hose attachment every now and then will keep this wall treatment free of dust. For larger stains, however, try a spray upholstery cleaner. It goes on foamy, and you just wipe it off with a towel.

Chapter 3

Flights of Fancy: Getting Creative with Canvas and Decoupage

LEVEL OF EASE: 3

ETW (ESTIMATED TIME OF WOW): 2 hours per panel

RECOMMENDED MUSIC: Pink Martini. *Hang on Little Tomato*

Everyone knows I'm a decoupage fiend. I will decoupage anything—cabinets, dining-room chairs, toilets—and if you stand still long enough, I will decoupage you. Now, I had always wanted to decoupage a wall, but the prospect seemed not only messy, but too permanent. Who wants all that glue and paper on the wall? So I came up with a technique that allows all the creativity of decoupage without the mess or long-term commitment.

Instead of working directly on the wall, you decoupage on sheets of canvas and when you're done, simply staple the sheets to the wall. It's easy to decoupage on canvas because it's so thick, and the nubby texture adds to the allure. And when you want to change the look of the room, just take the panels off the wall.

Because decoupage lends itself to an antique look, I went for a vintage European travelogue theme with travel stickers, postcards, florals, and old magazines. I created a series of love letters written by a fictional couple who meet during World War II, an American GI named Nick and a French woman named Mercedes. The combination of the graphics the and love letters makes the decoupage more than just a wall treatment—it's entertainment.

WHERE TO BUY IT

Make sure you buy canvas that's preprimed so it's ready to paint and decoupage. You'll find it in rolls at your local art supply store, where it's sold by the yard. You won't need a lot of canvas, since this project doesn't require you to cover the entire wall. Either an art supply store or an arts and crafts store will carry Mod Podge. I actually buy mine online because I can get larger quantities that way. I've listed a few of the Web sites that sell canvas and Mod Podge in the Resource Directory.

1 CUT THE CANVAS

First, decide how large you want your canvas sheets to be. I made the sheets around 30 inches wide, making the sheet behind the headboard wider to match its width. Each piece doesn't have to be the same size. To cut the canvas into your preferred widths, cut a little at the edge and tear the canvas apart with your bare hands. Besides making you feel very Neanderthal, this will create a more natural, rough edge instead of a scissor cut. And there's nothing like that satisfying ripping sound.

CLOSE ENOUGH

Part of the charm of these canvas sheets is that they are wrinkled and crooked. Do not worry if you have creases in the canvas because there's going to be even more wrinkling after you decoupage. Also, as you're tearing the canvas, don't stress about how straight you're tearing. This method creates remarkably straight lines, but the panels look even better when they're more free-form.

2 PAINT THE CANVAS

After cutting your canvas, paint each piece with interior latex paint. The paint will roll onto the canvas quite easily. I chose the same color as the wall, but a coordinating color will also look great. Be sure to use a drop cloth or plastic sheet so you don't make a mess.

3 LAY OUT YOUR ARTWORK

After the paint has dried overnight, lay out your papers on the canvas in the arrangement you want. Overlap images and vary the type of artwork you use.

Although I use glue and polyurethane for other decoupage projects, I prefer Mod Podge's all-in-one glue and sealer formulation for this wall treatment. It gets the job done in one step. Remove a few pieces of artwork at a time and apply a layer of Mod Podge on the canvas using an inexpensive, all-purpose paintbrush. Select a brush that's at least 3 inches wide, so you can cover a lot of surface area quickly. Place the papers back onto the wet canvas and add a layer of Mod Podge on top of them. Do this a section at a time until you've decoupaged the entire canvas sheet. Let the panel dry overnight. The Mod Podge goes on white, but it will become transparent as it dries. If you're attaching thicker pieces of paper, they may jut out slightly from the canvas as they dry. This is actually a splendid effect, because it adds a three-dimensional feel to the finished canvas.

HELPFUL HINT

Thinner papers will always wrinkle when you apply Mod Podge. I like the look of wrinkles, but if you want to avoid them, try photocopying your pictures at your local copier store. They use laser copy machines, which create colorfast images. Laser copy paper is very strong and decoupages with very few, if any, wrinkles. It's like Botox® for decoupage.

KEEPING IT CLEAN

The Mod Podge acts as an excellent sealer, so if you need to clean a spot on the panel, just use some household cleaner and a rag. Of course, any stains on the panel might contribute to its antiqued quality, so maybe you'd like to keep them. I always like an excuse for not cleaning.

5 STAPLE TO THE WALL

Using a staple gun, staple the top corners of the decoupaged panel to the wall. We're going for an impromptu look, so the corners don't even need to be perfectly straight. To that end, let the panels hang naturally, without stapling the bottoms.

Part II:
Metals of Honor

Outside of a nightclub or a creative work space, you don't usually see metal on a wall. But why not? It's stunning and surprisingly affordable, and lends itself to both modern and traditional spaces. Metal comes in many forms and finishes, and the following chapters just touch the surface. From aluminum roof flashing to blank compact discs, these unorthodox materials will open your eyes to what's possible in wall decor.

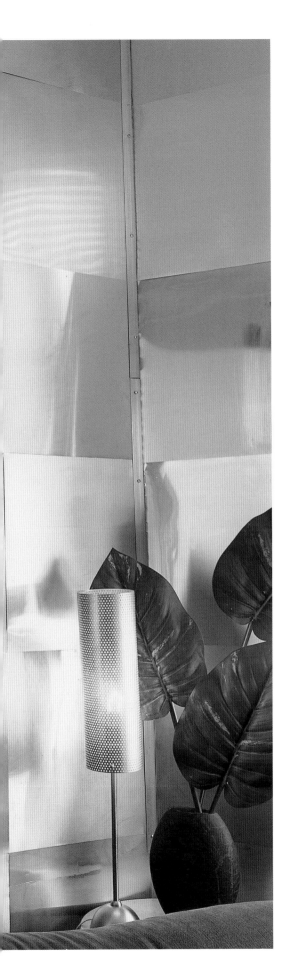

Chapter 4

Industrial Chic: The Modern Elegance of an Aluminum Grid

LEVEL OF EASE: (5)

ETW (ESTIMATED TIME OF WOW): 6 hours

RECOMMENDED MUSIC: Pet Shop Boys. *Behavior*

Here's a look that's anything but recycled. It's a metal grid that's actually squares of aluminum roof flashing, woven together in a checkerboard pattern. While the metal adds a high-tech touch to the wall, the overall design shines with sophistication.

Wait a minute. "Roof flashing?" you ask. "What's that?" Roof flashing is a roll of aluminum that's used to help waterproof your home. I love it because it's inexpensive and easy to work with.

To be honest, when I first set out to create this wall treatment for the den in my home, I wasn't sure how it would turn out. The procedure I had mapped out for myself seemed almost too easy. Surely something was going to go wrong. But it worked! As you'll see in the step-by-step instructions, once you get past the first four squares, you're on your way. I've had many people write to me, saying that they have successfully done this wall for their bedrooms, kitchens, and even hair salons.

WHERE TO BUY IT

You will find aluminum flashing in the roofing section of your local home improvement warehouse. It comes in rolls of 10 or 20 feet, in widths ranging from 6 to 20 inches. Measure the wall space you want to cover and then determine how many rolls you'll need to buy based on the square footage. For example, if your wall is 8 x 10 feet, you'll need at least 80 square feet of aluminum. It's a good idea to purchase more because you can always return the unused rolls. While you're at the home improvement warehouse, make a pit stop in the adhesive aisle and buy some tubes of paste adhesive. Make sure the package says it's good for adhering metal to surfaces. Again, buy a few extra tubes because you don't want to run out in the middle of the project. You can find a hacksaw for as little as $5 at the hardware store or home improvement warehouse.

1 CUT THE ALUMINUM PANELS

First, cut the aluminum into "squares," keeping one side an inch longer than the others. For example, if the coil is 10 inches wide, each panel will be 10 x 11 inches. Just unspool the coil and, using a straightedge as your guide, mark a line with a pen every 11 inches (or whatever your width is plus 1 inch). Using metal snips or a paper cutter, cut a straight line across your mark. What you will have then are panels with even edges (the existing edges of the aluminum) and two uneven ones (these are the sides you've just cut). The even edges are 1 inch longer than the uneven ones. Please note, even though I'm calling these sides "uneven," being hand-cut they are just uneven in comparison to the aluminum's machine-cut edges.

2 CLEAN THE PANELS

Your aluminum panels will probably have metal dust streaks on both sides. They come this way. Just wipe each side with a cotton cloth to remove the dust. You will notice that because the metal has been rolled in its packaging, the panels will be curved. You will be applying them on the wall so that the middle part curves out from the wall.

3 APPLY ADHESIVE TO THE EDGES

Apply a ribbon of adhesive along each uneven edge, about an inch from the edge. Do NOT apply adhesive along the even edges. Do this for each panel right before you apply it to the wall.

A paste adhesive like Liquid Nails works well because it holds quickly on the wall yet doesn't set permanently for about twenty minutes, so you can still move things around a bit. However, once it's set, this wall treatment is permanent.

4 APPLY THE PANELS TO THE WALL

Starting at the top corner of the wall, apply the first aluminum panel (Panel A), keeping the even, machine-cut edge flush against the ceiling and the uneven edge flush against the wall edge. Press firmly where the adhesive touches the wall until the panel holds firmly.

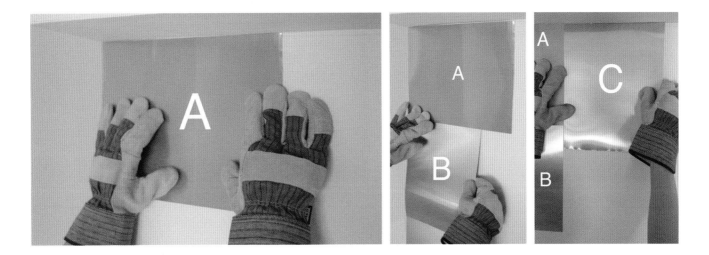

LET'S TAKE A BREAK

Are you following me? It sounds hard with all this even-uneven mumbo-jumbo, but all you have to remember is uneven edges are always tucked under the even edges. It's just like basket weaving. That's why earlier I said not to apply adhesive along the even edges. You need them clean so you can tuck the uneven edges under them.

Notice, too, that the metal has a natural grain to it. By weaving uneven edges under even ones, you will automatically be creating a checkerboard pattern with the alternating grains. Cool, huh?

On to the second panel (Panel B). You will put this below Panel A, which has an even bottom. Tuck about a half-inch of the uneven edge of Panel B under the bottom of the even edge of Panel A. Press firmly till this panel holds.

The third panel (Panel C) goes to the right of Panel A. Because the right edge of Panel A is uneven, you will be placing an even edge of Panel C on top of the uneven edge of Panel A. To determine where to line up this even edge, use the right edge of Panel B, which is even, as a guide.

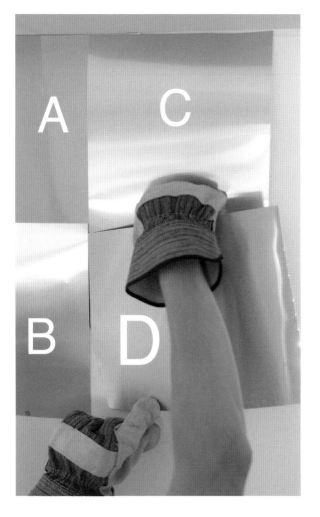

5 KEEP APPLYING THE PANELS

Next is the fourth panel (Panel D). You will notice that the right side of Panel B is even, while the bottom side of Panel C is uneven. Therefore, you will tuck an uneven edge of Panel D under the even edge of Panel B and overlap an even top edge of Panel D over the uneven bottom edge of Panel C.

Here is where you will appreciate how forgiving the adhesive is, because you can move the panels around so that the intersection of the four panels is perfectly straight.

Once you've done these first four panels, you can continue in any direction you wish, up and down or left to right. When you get to the bottom or end of the wall, your panels will probably be larger than the space that's left. No problem. Just measure the actual space you'll need and trim the panel to fit.

CLOSE ENOUGH

While you're progressing, it's likely that some of the panels will not be flush against the wall and bow out a bit. If this happens, congratulations. Any bends or imperfections will create more interesting reflections in the metal.

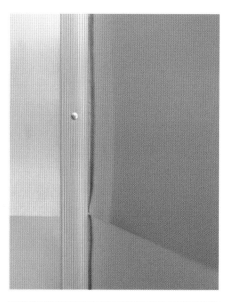

6 APPLY FINISHING TOUCHES TO CORNERS

When you get to the end of the wall, many of your edges will be uneven. To hide all the edges, nail in strips of metal carpet trim as molding. One-inch carpet trim comes in lengths of 3 or 6 feet, so for a standard wall height of 8 feet, you would use the 6-foot length and cut the 3-foot length with a hacksaw. The carpet trim comes with nails in the packaging, so just use those.

If you're not comfortable around tools, the idea of cutting metal with a hacksaw might sound frightening. Not to worry. A hacksaw is a small tool with small teeth that won't hurt you. If you're still afraid of having to cut the metal trim, don't cut it. Use the 6-foot piece and place a plant or a chair where the trim ends on the wall, and no one will know you didn't go all the way down to the floor. See, there are all kinds of little tricks.

7 APPLY FINISHING TOUCHES TO DOORS, WINDOWS, AND LIGHT SWITCHES

I wouldn't recommend using the carpet trim around windows and doors, because then you would have to cut the trim at angles so the pieces fit together at corners. Instead, just trim the panels with metal snips to make them as flush to the door and window frames as possible.

For light switches and outlets, use the metal snips to cut a hole for them and then install metallic plates to match.

After you're done with the entire wall, change into your hottest outfit, pour yourself a martini, and see how fabulous you look in the new room.

KEEPING IT SHINY

Over the years, aluminum reacts to the elements in the atmosphere and can become slightly cloudy in appearance. You won't even notice it unless you put a fresh piece of aluminum next to the older one. I had a painting on my aluminum wall, and when I removed the painting a few years later, there was a noticeable difference between the exposed metal and what was underneath the painting. I got the aluminum shiny again with a nonabrasive household cleaner like Formula 409®, rubbing it clean with a cotton cloth to get rid of any streaks.

Chapter 5

Wall of Sound: Styling with Blank Compact Discs

LEVEL OF EASE: 2

ETW (ESTIMATED TIME OF WOW): 8 hours

RECOMMENDED MUSIC: Meatloaf. *Bat Out of Hell*

In this age of MP3s and music downloads, what's to happen with good old compact discs? I know. Let's put them on the wall.

In this wall treatment, compact discs in clear jewel cases create a kaleidoscope of light and pattern that shifts according to the time of day and where you stand. From far away, the wall looks like glass blocks, subtly reflecting the light in the room. As you walk closer, the reflective CDs bounce colors and images to startling effect. Looking at the wall is mesmerizing, even hypnotic.

I created this wall for the conference room of a music management company, but it would also be ideal for a media room, a teenager's bedroom, or even a bathroom. And if you ever need a CD, you can just take it off the wall.

WHAT YOU'LL NEED

Blank CDs
Clear jewel cases
Laser level
Velcro™

WHERE TO BUY IT

Buy the blank CDs and jewel cases in bulk at an office supply store or home electronics warehouse, and you'll find it more economical. You'll also find great deals online if you do a search for "blank compact disks." Hey, you can even use those CDs that a certain Internet provider constantly sends.

1 DETERMINE HOW MANY CDS AND JEWEL CASES YOU'LL NEED

In case you're wondering, "jewel case" is a fancy name for the plastic cases CDs come in. They have nothing to do with diamonds, sorry. The standard size of a jewel case is 5 x 5-5/8 inches, so divide your wall width by 5-5/8 and you'll get the number you'll need for each row going across. Then divide your wall height in inches by 5, and you'll get the number you'll need for each vertical row. I used about five hundred CDs for this wall.

2 INSERT CDS INTO THEIR CASES

Place each blank CD in a jewel case so that the shiny side is facing out. Blank CDs come in a variety of colors, but I'm partial to silver. There's already enough color in the reflection of the surroundings and the prism effect of the CD.

3 CUT VELCRO INTO STRIPS

Buy rolls of Velcro and cut the Velcro into approximately 2-inch strips. A standard roll of Velcro is 15 feet long, which is 180 inches. You will need two 2-inch strips per CD, so buy accordingly.

4 PLACE VELCRO ON THE BACK

On the back side of the jewel case, attach two 2-inch strips of the fuzzy side of the Velcro so that they are completely within the boundaries of the CD. That way the Velcro remains hidden. Then add the spiky side of the Velcro to the fuzzy side with the adhesive side facing out, ready to stick on the wall. Frankly, this task is simple but terribly tiresome when you're talking hundreds of blank CDs, so get an eager assistant who doesn't know better, or the local Boy Scout troop, to help you.

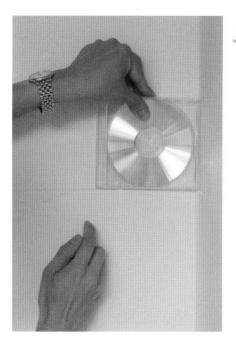

5 LINE UP YOUR FIRST CD ON THE WALL

The most challenging part of this wall treatment is lining the CDs up straight. But it's easy using a laser level and the straight edges of the jewel case. I use a laser level for many of the projects in this book. If you've never used a laser level, go out and buy one—you'll love it! Using either removable sticky paste or air suction, a laser level clings to the wall and shines a straight line horizontally or vertically. Just shine the laser level along the width of the wall and line up the jewel case along the laser line. In the photograph, I'm lining up the bottom edge of the jewel case with the laser line, but you can also line up the top edge. Take a pre-Velcroed CD case and press it onto the wall until the adhesive sticks. If you follow the laser line, you should be fine. However, if you make mistakes in positioning, just peel off the CD from the wall. The spiky side of the Velcro stays on the wall, and you can just reposition the CD on it.

CLOSE ENOUGH

If you have windows or art to work around, the CDs work really well because they can border these objects easily. Just don't expect them to butt right up against them because the measurements will never be that exact. There will be a blank border, but it will look like you planned it that way.

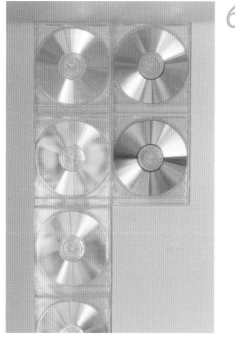

6 ADD CDS HORIZONTALLY AND VERTICALLY

Start at one side of the wall and do one row at a time. Use the straight edge of adjacent jewel cases to help you line up the CDs vertically. Every now and then, use the level to make sure you're placing the CDs on the wall straight.

When you're done, the wall will look like it is dancing with light. So join in and do a little dance of completion. But not too long. You have to make "CD-Velcroing" badges for all those Boy Scouts.

KEEPING IT CLEAN

The CDs in their jewel cases are very easy to clean with a damp cloth. And since they're attached to the wall with Velcro, you can easily replace individual jewel cases that get dirty or scuffed.

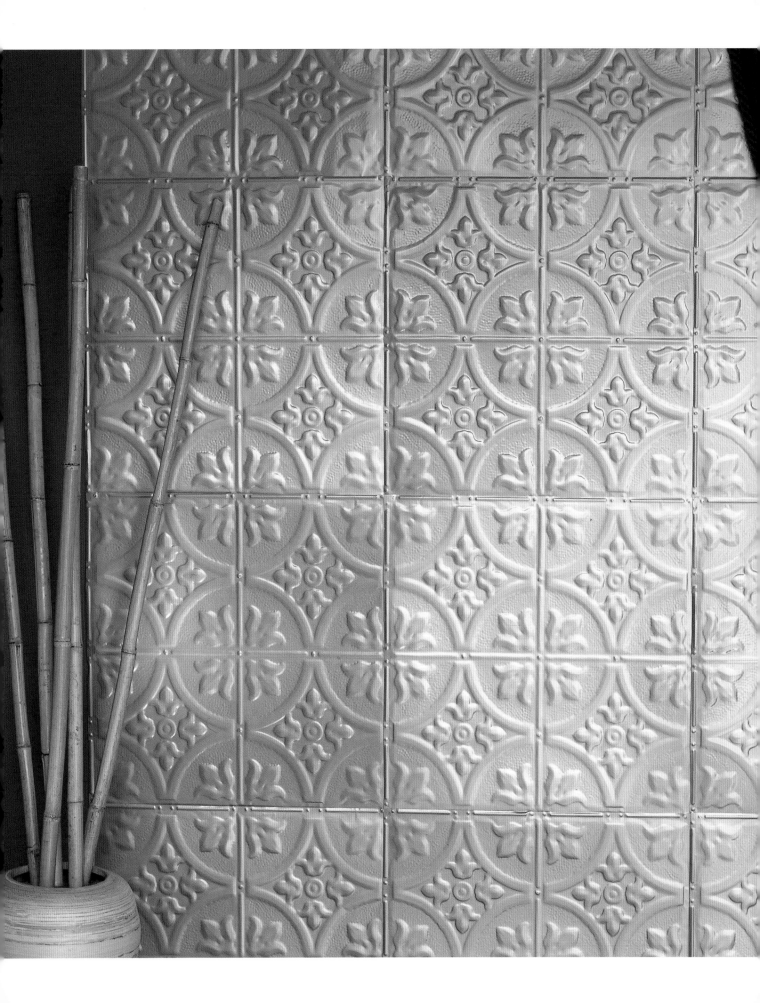

Chapter 6

Staring at the Ceiling: Going Rococo with Tin Ceiling Panels

LEVEL OF EASE: 3

ETW (ESTIMATED TIME OF WOW): 2 hours

RECOMMENDED MUSIC: Josh Groban. *Closer*

One of the pleasures of older buildings is the architectural detail absent in modern spaces. While the mid-twentieth century gave us that oh so lovely feature known as cottage cheese ceilings, the nineteenth century introduced the architectural marvel of tin ceilings. Many older buildings still boast these original ceilings, with their ornate patterns and aged patinas. When you look up and see these gilded wonders, you may think of fanciful turn-of-the-century balls attended by society women in sumptuous gowns.

But just because they're called "tin ceiling panels" doesn't mean they need to stay there. You can use tin panels on a foyer wall to create a dramatic entrance, behind a bed as an elaborate headboard, or even in a kitchen to give it an old-world feel. Today, tin ceiling panels are being reproduced in myriad patterns and finishes, so they can match any decor, from Art Deco to Tuscan. Now let's hope that cottage cheese ceilings don't make a big comeback.

WHERE TO BUY IT

There are several online sources for tin ceiling panels, which come in a standard size of 2 x 2 feet. I've named some of the manufacturers in the Resource Directory. Depending on the finish of the panel, prices range from $8 to $20 per panel.

1 DECIDE HOW MANY PANELS YOU'LL NEED

If you have a standard 8-foot ceiling, you will want to use three or four panels vertically. How wide you want to go is up to you. However, I do not recommend covering an entire wall. Not only is the effect overwhelming on such a large scale; more importantly, you will most likely be working around windows, doors, and electrical outlets. Tin ceiling panels are easy to cut with metal snips, but the cut edges are notoriously sharp, so try to use them whole. You'll find that even a 6-foot-wide section of tin panels (for example, three panels wide) will create quite a dramatic effect.

2 APPLY ADHESIVE TO THE BACK

Squeeze some paste adhesive on the back of each ceiling panel. Besides bonding the panels to the wall, the adhesive helps the panels stay in place as you are nailing them. You'll be putting up one ceiling panel at a time, so apply the adhesive right before you're ready to nail it up.

HELPFUL HINT

Although I used regular nails in this demonstration, upholstery nails work particularly well for this wall treatment because the nail heads are so much larger than the holes in the panels. Also, they're beautiful and come in various finishes and styles.

3 NAIL THE PANELS FROM LEFT TO RIGHT

You will notice that the ceiling panels have a nail hole near each of their four corners. The holes are predrilled to line up both vertically and horizontally with adjacent ceiling panels. You will be starting with the top left panel, going from left to right. Use a laser level to make sure that the top edges of your panels are straight (see page 41 for instructions on how to use a laser level). However, if your panels are going flush to the ceiling, you won't need the level. Finish the top row before you move on to the next row. This sequence is helpful because you will be overlapping panels, moving from the left to the right. In the first ceiling panel, hammer a nail into the upper left hole.

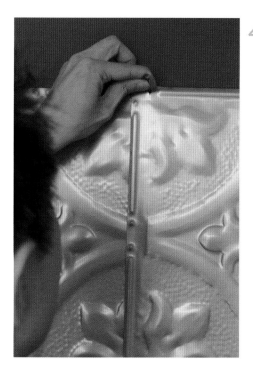

4 KEEP GOING

Overlap the adjacent ceiling panel so its upper left hole lines up with the first panel's upper right hole. Then hammer a nail through both of these holes.

CLOSE ENOUGH

As you're working with the ceiling panels, you will inevitably bend the edges, and they won't have the pristine out-of-the-box look anymore. No problem. First of all, who wants that pristine look anyway? We're pretending you got these tin ceiling panels from an estate sale in a New England brownstone. On a practical level, if the edges have bent out and you're afraid of snagging your grocery bags on them, just take a hammer and smash them down. The edges will be flat again, and they will look even more aged.

5 HAMMER THE NEXT ROW

When you move on to the next row, you will be overlapping vertically adjacent edges. Make sure the holes line up and put a nail through them. Remember, there's always one nail for every two overlapping holes.

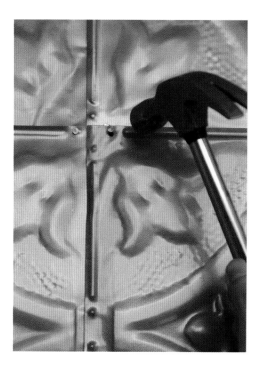

HELPFUL HINT

Your wall section with tin ceiling panels will look great on its own, but try framing it with accents to soften the look. Remember that this wall treatment can be visually overwhelming with the shiny finish, ornate pattern, and bright color, so any elements you can add to accessorize the wall will create a more harmonious feel. Try draping fabric along one edge or placing a bookcase or large plant along another.

KEEPING IT CLEAN

Because the tin ceiling panels are not flat, dust can quickly settle in the grooves and patterns. A weekly dusting will go far in keeping them nice and shiny. A damp cloth will remove any additional stains, but go over the area with a dry cloth to make sure you have no streaks.

Chapter 7

The Latest Bulletin: Chicken Wire Turns Your Wall into a Message Center

LEVEL OF EASE: ②

ETW (ESTIMATED TIME OF WOW): 2 hours

RECOMMENDED MUSIC: Dolly Parton. *Little Sparrow*

I was visiting a friend not too long ago for a spoon-bending party (that's a whole other story and book) and saw that she had made an ingenious frame for photographs—a small piece of chicken wire placed on the wall with clips for photos. I immediately knew I could do this on a larger scale and cover an entire wall with the chicken wire. It creates a shimmering canvas that doubles as both a place to hang pictures and a bulletin board. What a great look for an office, studio, or craft room.

Everyone who has seen this wall treatment has wanted to make it. The photographer for this book actually absconded with my surplus materials so she could duplicate the effect in her home. (And then her father took some of her extra wire and did the wall himself.) No wonder, because not only does it look great with its soft waves of metal, but it's also so functional. You'll actually want to make more to-do lists to fill up this wall-sized bulletin board. Okay, maybe that's an exaggeration.

Clothespins or electrical clips
General-purpose leather
    work gloves
Goggles (recommended)
Hardware cloth
Metal snips
Plastic clamps
Screwdriver
Screws

WHERE TO BUY IT

You can find everything for this project at your local hardware store or home improvement warehouse. The hardware cloth, the clamps, the metal snips, the electrical clips, the clothespins—they're all under one roof. (Why do I sound like a TV commercial?)

1 UNROLL THE CHICKEN WIRE

Although I call it chicken wire, the real name of what you should buy is "hardware cloth," which is strange since it's neither hardware nor cloth. You will find it next to the chicken wire. While chicken wire has hexagonal holes, hardware cloth has rectangular holes, giving it a clean industrial feel rather than a farmhouse feel. Not that there's anything wrong with that. I will use both terms interchangeably. Hardware cloth comes in rolls of various lengths. I prefer the 10-foot length because it's easier to manage and will work well for a standard 8-foot-high wall.

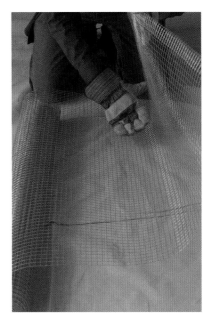

First, unroll the hardware cloth and flatten it out. Make sure you wear goggles and gloves as you do this, because unrolling the hardware cloth is similar to wrestling an alligator. It wants to get away from you, and it will bite. Having someone's assistance as you roll it out will definitely help. As you unroll the cloth, bend it the opposite way and step on it so it flattens.

CLOSE ENOUGH

You will never get the chicken wire perfectly flat, no matter how hard you try. Having been rolled up at the hardware store since the dawn of time, it will naturally curl, even where you've flattened it. Just think of that as a good thing, because the waves add visual interest to the wall. And where it curls out from the wall, you will find it easier to clip your photos and messages.

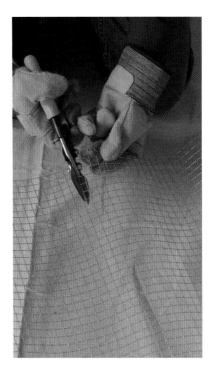

2 CUT THE CHICKEN WIRE

After it's flattened, trim it with metal snips to the length you want. You can make it any size. It looks great from floor to ceiling, but if you have a desk and cabinets against the wall, you may only want to cover the top section of your wall.

3 BEND THE EDGES

The edges at the top and bottom where you've cut your chicken wire will have very sharp points. Wearing leather work gloves, bend the edges over to hide them.

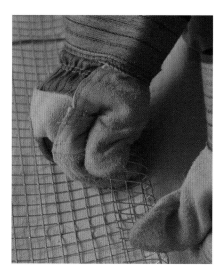

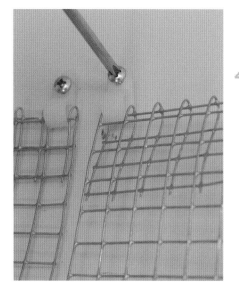

4 FASTEN THE WIRE TO THE WALL

You will use plastic clamps to fasten the chicken wire to the wall. These plastic clamps are usually found in the electrical department of the hardware store. Wrap the clamp around one of the wires on the top, place a screw through the holes and screw the clamp to the wall to hold the wire. Use two clamps on the top of the chicken wire, and two clamps on the bottom to hold the piece in place. Again, get someone to help you hold up the chicken wire as you attach the screws. Place another sheet of chicken wire next to the first and attach it to the wall the same way.

5 ATTACH PHOTOS AND NOTES

When you've put up all the chicken wire you desire, the fun starts. Using clothespins or electrical clips, affix notes, photos, or whatever onto the chicken wire. If you ever decide to take down this wall treatment, you can reuse the materials to raise rabbits, or keep the fox out of the henhouse.

KEEPING IT CLEAN

In the event of dust or the occasional cobweb (not that you would ever have them, my friend), a quick vacuum with the upholstery attachment will freshen up this project very nicely. Of course, you should remove any notes or photographs from the wall first.

Part III:
Special Effects

I like to think of every room as if it were a set in a movie or a stage in a play. The best set design transports you to a particular time or place, creates a mood, tells a story, or all of the above. This heightened theatricality is what I've aimed for in the following walls. Their unusual elements define spaces that are breathtakingly beautiful, sometimes skating on the edge of reality.

Chapter 8

Branching Out: Bamboo Branches Bring the Outdoors In

LEVEL OF EASE: 1

ETW (ESTIMATED TIME OF WOW): 2 hours

RECOMMENDED MUSIC: Enya. *A Day Without Rain*

Listed in my eighth-grade yearbook next to my class photo is the profession I thought I wanted to pursue at that tender age: botanist. I had no idea why I wanted to be a botanist, except that I was fascinated by flowers and plants. However, as one of the few Asians who is horrible at math and science, I never did become a botanist. Still, my love of botanicals never waned, and as a designer I am particularly fascinated by tree branches. A simple branch, gnarled and extending its fingers outward, exudes such quiet beauty, so it was only natural that I would want to create an entire wall of branches, as if they were growing in suspended animation. But what kind of branches would I use, and where would I find them?

I thought I had hit the mother lode one morning when I heard the buzzing noise of tree trimmers cutting back the ficus trees that grow on my block. While the workers weren't looking, I secretly grabbed an armful and deposited them in my backyard. As they dried and shed their leaves, though, the branches did not have much character to them. Then one day as I was wandering through a craft store, I came upon the perfect branches: bamboo spray. They have a beautiful rust color, and the twigs splay elegantly. Best of all, they're flat, so they rest right up against the wall without jabbing anyone in the eye. This wall treatment is truly one of my favorites. And you won't believe how easily the branches affix to the wall.

Bamboo spray branches
Power drill and 1/16-inch
    drill bits
Hammer
Small nails

WHERE TO BUY IT

Like I said, I found these branches at a craft store. Go to your local craft store, or any home furnishings store that has a silk and dried floral department. Even if you don't find these exact branches, chances are you will have a choice of several beautiful alternatives.

1 DRILL TWO HOLES IN EACH BRANCH

Before embarking on this wall treatment, I considered several ways to attach the branches. Maybe I'd tie wire around the branches and screw the wires into the wall. Maybe large staples at strategic points. Maybe a hot-glue gun. But the method I selected turned out to be easier than I even imagined.

Using a 1/16-inch drill bit, drill two holes in each branch—one near the thick base and one closer to the top in the skinnier section. At first, I was afraid that the drill would crack the branches, but it didn't. The bamboo is so hard that it can withstand the drill, even where it's thin. If you want to make sure that the bamboo doesn't break, drill at one of the joints where the branch is thicker.

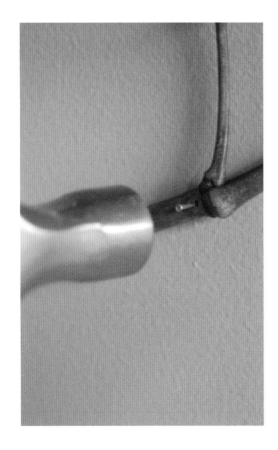

2 NAIL THE FIRST BRANCH

Choose nails that are narrow enough to fit the predrilled hole, yet long enough to secure the branch to the wall. The head of the nail should also be larger than the drill hole. I used brass escutcheon nails.

Start at the lower-left-hand corner of the wall. Insert a small nail in each of the predrilled holes and nail the branch to the wall. After the first nail, the branch will already be solidly attached. The second nail just helps keep it in place. Although the branches are flat, a branch may occasionally bow out in the middle. If that's the case, turn the branch around so that the nail holes are flush against the wall.

3 START FANNING OUT BRANCHES

After nailing the first branch, it's time to add more branches. All subsequent branches should look like they grow out of a branch that's already on the wall. You never want a branch floating by itself, so take the base of the new branch and butt it up against the base of the first branch. Nail this second branch with two nails. Keep extending the branches, building on previous ones. Overlap some branches so part of the wall is fuller while making other sections sparser.

CLOSE ENOUGH

If a branch still looks like it's floating because you didn't nail it right next to another one, you can hide the gaps when you start overlapping branches. Also, you'll be adding elements to the branches later to further hide the holes.

4 ADD FLOWERS OR LEAVES

Because the twigs in the branches are dense, especially when you overlap them, you can easily slide silk flowers or leaves between them. Perhaps change the ornamentation depending on the seasons, so that in the fall there are autumn leaves, in the winter a few artificial snowflakes, and in spring and summer beautiful blossoms. Don't worry that your bamboo branches are a different species from the flowers you choose. Since I never did become a botanist, I'd never notice the discrepancy.

ANOTHER IDEA

Instead of flowers or leaves, you can use the branches to hold greeting cards during the holidays, or as an organic bulletin board for photographs and notes.

KEEPING IT CLEAN

These branches are thin and won't accumulate much dust. If you do feel like cleaning them, a feather duster would be more than sufficient. And if a few feathers get caught on the branches, they'd probably look pretty good. As an alternative, a can of compressed gas will also blow away the dust. (Plus, they're so much fun to use.) Just be sure to remove any flowers or leaves first or they'll fly everywhere.

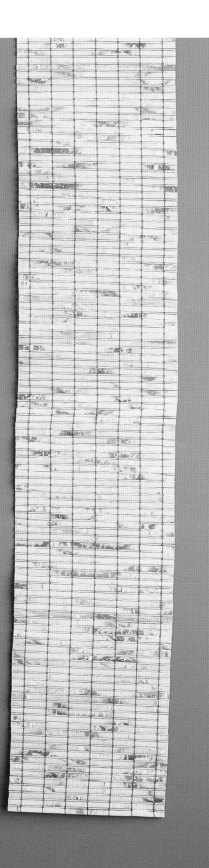

Chapter 9

Afterglow: Free-floating Candles for a Tranquil Retreat

LEVEL OF EASE: 4

ETW (ESTIMATED TIME OF WOW): 3 hours

RECOMMENDED MUSIC: Sarah Brightman. *Eden*

My friend, interior designer Laurie Faulkner, likes to take me to hip, new restaurants so we can be inspired by the decor. I find that restaurants are now the harbingers of interior design trends, much as hotels were a few years ago. One trend I'm seeing a lot of in restaurants is the use of candles. They seem to be everywhere, lined up on shelves, illuminating each table, or acting as a focal point on the bar. I swear, some restaurants have so many candles, they look like the Phantom of the Opera's underground lair. At the Chinese restaurant my family owned, the only time we ever lit candles was when we had a power blackout.

The appeal of candles is understandable, though. It provides soft light that's romantic, adding an air of elegance to any environment. And the lighting is extremely flattering. So, of course, I just had to create a wall of candlelight. It's an especially dramatic backdrop for a dining room, bedroom, foyer, or meditation area. Rather than sitting on shelves, the candles float across the wall, accompanied by a row of silk roses that punch up the drama.

Drill bit for metal
Glass votives and candles
Power drill and drill bits
    (with at least 14 volts)
Screwdriver
Screws
Sheet of paper or masking tape
Silk roses
Test tubes (20mm x 150mm)
3/4-inch copper tube straps
2-inch copper tube caps

WHERE TO BUY IT

I looked everywhere for something affordable and unique to hold the candles, and I found it, of all places, in the hardware store. There, accompanied by an angelic chorus (actually the beeping of forklifts) was the answer to my prayers: copper tube caps. They are meant to go at the end of copper pipes; but at 2 inches in diameter, they're the perfect size to fit a glass votive. And the copper finish adds a beautiful design element to the mix. In the same aisle are the copper straps for the test tubes. Speaking of test tubes, you'll find them at most educational supply stores or, better yet, at an online scientific supply store. I've listed some in the Resource Directory.

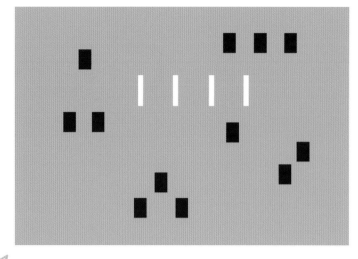

1 DRAW A DIAGRAM

On a piece of paper (or on the actual wall with masking tape), indicate where you will place your votives. The diagram above illustrates my game plan, with the black boxes indicating the votives and the white rectangles representing the test tubes. As you can see, I planned an assymetrical placement because it's more visually interesting. But there's a correct method to being assymetrical. You don't just scatter the votives everywhere. The key to being assymetrical is grouping the votives in singles, pairs, and trios. At the same time, make room for the flower tubes. Instead of scattering the flowers, keep them together as a unit.

2 DRILL HOLES IN THE COPPER TUBE CAPS

First, each copper cap needs to be drilled with a hole so it can be screwed to the wall. Drilling a hole in metal? Am I out of my mind? I admit, I am scared of power tools that involve sharp, pointy corkscrews; but I was determined, and bought a metal drill bit that fit my electric drill. Unfortunately, my cordless drill did not have the power to go through the metal. I needed a power drill with at least fourteen volts of power, so I called my handyman friend to do it for me. He drilled holes in a dozen caps in two minutes flat. The lesson of this story? Get the proper tools or, better yet, get someone with the right power tool to drill the holes for you. I'm all about delegating.

3 SCREW THE COPPER CAPS INTO THE WALL

Predrill a hole in the wall where each copper tube cap will go. So that the screw fits snugly into the predrilled hole, select a drill bit that is one size smaller than the screw you will be using. When predrilling, angle your bit slightly downward, since the rim of the cap will force you to drill the screw at the same downward angle. Then insert your screw in the hole at the same downward angle. Make sure that you choose a screw whose head is larger than the hole in the copper cap.

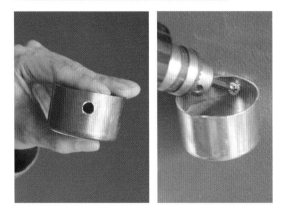

4 INSERT GLASS VOTIVES

A glass votive fits snugly in the copper cap. (Actually, is a votive the actual candle or the container that holds the candle? I can never get the distinction.) Anyway, don't put a candle directly into the copper cap. It will melt into the cap and make a mess.

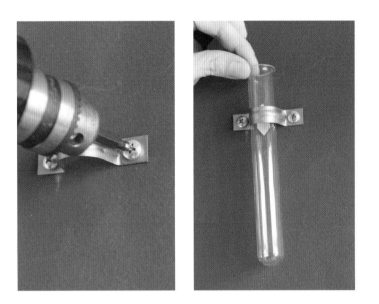

5 SCREW COPPER TUBE STRAPS INTO THE WALL

Three-quarter-inch copper tube straps, used for securing pipes, are in the same aisle in the hardware store as the copper caps. They are the perfect size to hold a test tube. Each strap already has a screw hole on either side, so just insert the screws.

However, don't tighten the screws all the way. First, slide a test tube into the opening, and then tighten just enough to hold the test tube at the rim.

6 INSERT SILK ROSES

Insert a single silk rose into each test tube. You'll probably need to trim the stem so the rose isn't sticking out too far. If you'd prefer, fill the test tubes with water and use real roses, but I like the no-maintenance feature of the artificial ones.

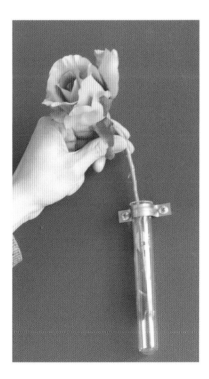

KEEPING IT CLEAN

The test tubes will get dusty, so remove them every month and place them in your dishwasher. As for the copper tube caps holding the votives, they will naturally oxidize, especially when you put your fingers on them. I like this natural patina. But if you want to make them shiny again, just wipe them with a diluted solution of CLR® Enhanced Calcium, Lime & Rust Remover and water.

Chapter 10

A Novel Idea: The Pages of a Book Seem to Fly Away

LEVEL OF EASE: 1

ETW (ESTIMATED TIME OF WOW): 1 hour

RECOMMENDED MUSIC: *Xanadu* Soundtrack

I'm the biggest Olivia Newton-John fan in the world. As such, I am one of the three people who saw *Xanadu*, her ahead-of-its-time roller disco musical. In the movie, Olivia plays a muse from Mount Olympus who's frozen in a wall mural on Venice Beach. The opening musical number begins with pieces of paper flying in the wind, traveling for miles until they land in front of the mural, bringing Olivia magically to life.

This classic movie scene inspired this wall treatment, in which it appears that a sudden guest of wind has opened a storybook and scattered its pages through the air. The image is romantic and whimsical, and you can imagine the pages flying off to new lands and adventures. I also love the simplicity of this wall. With just a few randomly placed pages, you create a dynamic effect. But I'm still waiting for Olivia to appear.

A used novel
Stapler
X-Acto® knife

WHERE TO BUY IT

The most important step in this wall treatment is finding the right novel to use. I do not advocate the defacing of books, so please no new books, library books, and certainly no books from my wonderful publisher Watson-Guptill. Go to a thrift store and find a nice used book that many people have already had the pleasure of reading. If the book is a little worn and yellow, that's even better.

1 REMOVE SOME PAGES

Using an X-Acto knife, randomly cut pages from the binding. Remove pages from different parts of the book, so there is not a visible gap. Also, select a variety of page types, for example, beginnings of chapters, all type, and illustrations. Start with about thirty pages; you can always cut out more.

2 STAPLE THE PAGES TO THE WALL

Using a regular stapler, staple the pages to the wall. The pages should be turned at different angles, upside down, and forward.

3 GIVE THEM MOVEMENT

Staple a few of the pages on the bottom so they droop over. Clump some together and isolate others.

4 MAKE ONE PAGE FLY OUT OF THE BOOK

Place the open book on a nearby table or bookshelf. Staple one of the pages to the wall just above the book, allowing the bottom of the page to touch the book. The page will appear to be flying out of the book this very instant.

ANOTHER IDEA

Another idea for this wall is to substitute sheet music for the book pages. Place a music book on a stand and have the pages flying out of it.

CLOSE ENOUGH

Don't worry about the placement of the storybook pages. Go free. You can't make a mistake. Remember, it's supposed to be the wind moving these pages, and wind is not anal-retentive.

KEEPING IT CLEAN

Over time, the pages may gather dust, so shake the pages now and then to remove any dust. Feel free to replace the pages periodically, too, and vary the wall placement. You won't see the little staple holes on the wall, and it's fun to see the pages flying differently.

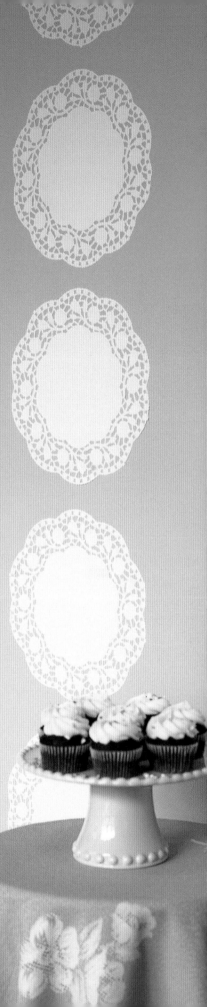

Part IV:
Pulp Power

Paper is rather low on the pecking order of design elements, but it is one of the most versatile materials around. It's lightweight, cuts easily, and comes in a gazillion colors, textures, and patterns. From wrapping paper to corrugated cardboard and envelopes, these Pulp Power wall treatments explore the exciting possibilities of this underrated material. If you thought paper meant only wallpaper, think again.

Chapter 11

Out of the Box: The Natural Simplicity of Corrugated Cardboard

LEVEL OF EASE: 4

ETW (ESTIMATED TIME OF WOW): 2 hours

RECOMMENDED MUSIC: Aimee Mann. *Bachelor No. 2*

I love corrugated cardboard. Ever since I was a little boy making forts out of scrap cardboard (forts that were impeccably decorated, mind you), I could see the potential in this utilitarian material. Take a closer look at it and you'll see why it's so wonderful. The color is rich and earthy. It feels nice to the touch. And the corrugated lines, each perfectly formed, resemble sunburnt knolls and . . . oh, don't get me started.

This stunning wall treatment really shows off the best qualities of cardboard. Strips are woven together like a piecrust, and the corrugation provides horizontal or vertical lines, depending on how the cardboard is hanging, to create a checkerboard pattern. After demonstrating this wall treatment on HGTV, I got calls from people saying it was a great way to cover up an ugly wall that they didn't want to paint. Now, that's what I call thinking outside the box.

1 CHOOSE A WIDTH FOR YOUR CARDBOARD

Corrugated cardboard comes in rolls of various widths, from 6 inches on up, and the rolls are 250 feet long. The technical name for it is b-flute corrugated rolls; the "b-flute" refers to the size of the corrugation. I'm holding the 24-inch-wide roll, which is a good size because you can easily cut it to whatever width you'd like. Also, most walls are 96 inches high, so the 24-inch roll allows for exactly four strips up and down.

2 CUT THE ROLL INTO STRIPS

Cut the roll of cardboard into strips that will hang vertically. How many strips will you need? Suppose your wall is 96 inches high by 140 inches wide. Divide 140 inches by 24 and you get 5.8, so you will cut six strips that are 96 inches long. Then cut the roll into strips that will hang horizontally. Since the wall is 96 inches high, you will need exactly four strips that are 140 inches long. For fire protection, it's a good idea to spray all the cardboard strips with a flame retardant first before placing them on the wall.

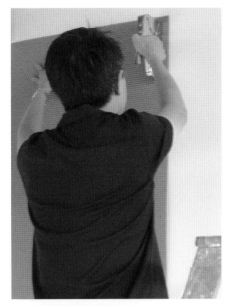

3 STAPLE THE FIRST VERTICAL STRIP

Using a staple gun, staple the vertical cardboard strips first. Going from left to right, start with the first strip. Hold the strip up to the top of the wall and staple the cardboard at the top left and top right.

4 STAPLE THE SECOND VERTICAL STRIP

On the second vertical strip, however, you will staple it to the wall at a lower point, about 27 inches down (as long as it's past 24 inches). This strip will therefore droop down.

5 ALTERNATE THE STAPLING PATTERN

On the third strip, staple at the top, and the fourth, staple lower down (again, about 27 inches down). What you will get is drooping cardboard strips on every other row.

HELPFUL HINT

Now, it is more than likely that your last vertical strip at the end of the wall will not be exactly 24 inches because wall widths are not made in increments of twenty-four. If they were, there would be a political thriller written about the mathematical and religious implications of number twenty-four. But that's okay. Just cut the strip to fit. Cardboard is so easy to work with.

6 WEAVE THE HORIZONTAL STRIPS

Once all the vertical strips are stapled in place, you can start weaving the horizontal strips over and under the vertical ones. Place the horizontal strip on top of the first vertical strip—lining up the top and left edges of the horizontal strip with the top and left edges of the vertical strip—and staple both into place along the top edge.

Then tuck the horizontal strip under the second vertical strip (which is drooping) and staple them both to the wall along the top edge as I'm gracefully doing in the photograph (below, right). Now you'll know why we had every other vertical row droop—so we could weave the strips under those pieces. Believe me, it helps to have someone hold the horizontal strips up with you. Otherwise, you can disappear under the cardboard and not be found for days.

After you've woven the top horizontal strip, the subsequent horizontal strips are much easier to install. Just keep weaving them under and over. When a horizontal strip is under a vertical strip, hold the vertical strip up so that it's out of the way and staple the horizontal strip. This way the staple is hidden underneath the vertical strip. When a horizontal strip is on top of a vertical strip, you don't need to staple it there; only staple when it will be hidden by a vertical strip. Of course, you will staple the far left and far right edges of the horizontal strips to keep them in place.

CLOSE ENOUGH

When I first attempted this wall treatment, I found that I had cut the strips too short, because I had not allowed for the extra inches required in the weaving over and under. So the strip did not extend the length of the wall. This could happen to you. But no worries. Just cut a short piece that you can add to the end. Because the cardboard is woven over and under, the short piece can start under, and no one will know that it's not one continuous piece. This wall treatment is very forgiving that way. If you make any mistakes or you happen to fling spaghetti sauce on it during a food fight, you can cut that part out and insert a new segment of cardboard.

7 PROTECT THE OUTLETS

If there are electrical outlets on the wall, it is very easy to cut a hole in the cardboard for it. Apply electrical tape to the edges so there is no exposed cardboard.

KEEPING IT CLEAN

As I've already said, if you get a stain on any part of the cardboard, you can cut that section out and replace it with a new piece. Therefore, it's a good idea to keep some extra cardboard on hand. A quick dusting will also clean any dust that settles in the grooves of the cardboard.

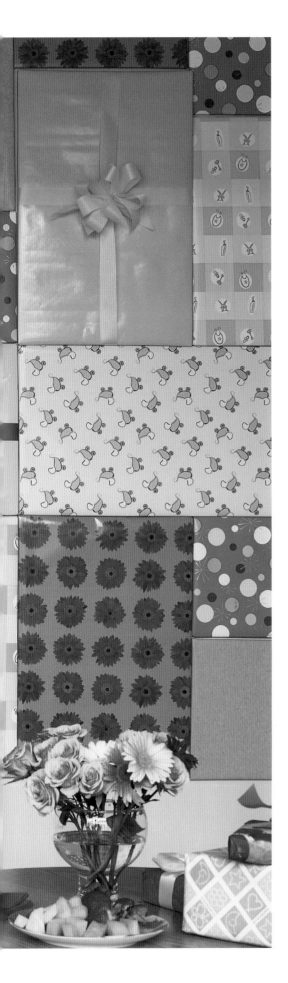

Chapter 12

It's a Wrap: A Collage of Wrapped Presents Marks the Occasion

LEVEL OF EASE: 3

ETW (ESTIMATED TIME OF WOW): 6 hours

RECOMMENDED MUSIC: Abba. *Gold*

Everyone loves presents. Whenever my dog, Broadway, sees a wrapped present, she assumes it's for her and will sit and guard the package for hours. She won't even tear the wrapping off. Broadway's just happy to sit there, imagining all the goodies hidden underneath the paper. Needless to say, Broadway loves this wall.

This wall treatment is specifically designed for parties, holidays, and special occasions. It's a collage of brightly wrapped "gift boxes" that can adorn an entryway, or the wall behind a buffet or gift table. Pieces of foam core are wrapped with colorful papers and attached to the wall with dabs of museum putty. When the occasion is over, just take them down. Then you can save the pieces of foam core and rewrap them in a different-themed wrapping paper for another occasion. I first did a wall for Christmas, put the foam core away in the closet for a year, and then resurrected it for a baby shower. It's the wall that keeps on giving.

WHERE TO BUY IT

As I mentioned in Chapter 1,
foam core sheets are available
at art supply stores. There you
can also find museum putty,
which is available in hardware
stores and stores that sell
household goods as well.

1 DIVIDE THE FOAM CORE INTO PANELS

First, measure your wall to determine how much foam core you'll
need to purchase. A standard sheet of foam core is 32 x 40 inches, so
just a few sheets will usually be enough. Within each foam core sheet,
decide on the pattern of shapes that will become the wrapped gift
boxes. Vary the patterns. Try squares, rectangles, vertical boxes, horizontal boxes, big ones, and small ones. Write letters and/or numbers
on each "box," and draw this configuration on a separate piece of
paper so you can remember how the pieces fit back together. Then
using a straightedge and an X-Acto knife, cut the foam core into the
corresponding boxes on a cutting mat. To be extra safe, wear an
oven mitt on the hand that is holding the straightedge (see "Helpful
Hint" on page 17 for instructions on cutting foam core).

Besides writing numbers and letters on the front of each panel, also
write them on the back. That way, after you wrap the panel, you still
know where it's supposed to go on the wall. Be sure to write the numbers and letters in the correct up-and-down direction so you don't put
the boxes up sideways later.

2 WRAP THE PANELS

Next, wrap each foam core panel with the wrapping paper, securing
the paper with tape. You only need to extend the paper around the
back by a half-inch, since no one will be seeing the back. Also, you will
want to allow room on the back to place your museum putty adhesive.

As you wrap each present, keep track of which paper you're using for
the surrounding presents. Try to spread the patterns evenly around the
wall. Also, add a bow to a few random panels to add to the merriment
of the occasion.

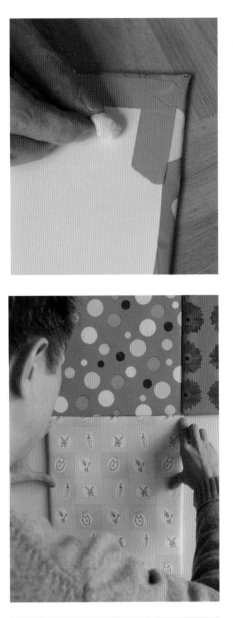

3 ADHERE WITH PUTTY

Put a little ball of putty in the corners and along the sides of each panel. Museum putty is designed to keep breakable items from shifting on bookshelves, but I've found it to be a great adhesive for lightweight objects. Just be sure that you're using fresh putty out of the package. Once you've used it once, the adhesive qualities diminish, at least when it comes to sticking things on the wall. I used to use poster putty, which is actually meant for wall hangings; but museum putty is stickier, and in this case stickier is better since we want to make sure the panels stay up. For larger foam core pieces, you will need larger amounts of putty.

Then push the wrapped foam core panels onto the wall according to your predetermined template. Press firmly where the putty meets the wall.

HELPFUL HINT

As much as I love foam core, the main problem with it is that it warps. When that happens, an entire side or corner can bend away from the wall, causing the putty to lose contact with it. Then that "gift" can fall down. The solution is to show that foam core who's boss. Bend the foam core in the opposite direction, even crack it, so the warped side makes contact with the wall again. You will get an ugly crack line on your foam core, but it doesn't matter because it's covered with wrapping paper anyway. Unlike real presents, what's underneath the wrapping paper is nobody's business.

4 REMOVE THEM AFTER THE OCCASION

When you remove the panels, there may be some putty stuck to the wall. Peel it off with your fingernails or use a larger piece of putty to remove it. If for some reason there is some oily residue left from the putty, follow the directions on the package to clean it. Store the panels in a closet for a future use. They will store flat, so they won't take up that much room. If you want, Broadway can guard them for you.

KEEPING IT CLEAN

If, while the panels are up, one gets stained by, say, a wayward splash of eggnog, just remove the panel and rewrap it. Wall treatments that come in sections are awfully convenient, aren't they?

Chapter 13

Hip to Be Square: Paper Tiles with a Three-Dimensional Twist

LEVEL OF EASE: (1)

ETW (ESTIMATED TIME OF WOW): 2 hours

RECOMMENDED MUSIC: Weezer. *Green Album*

I have nothing against wallpaper. In fact, these days wallpaper comes in the most wonderful colors and textures. I just don't like applying it. All that mess with the paste, a squeegee, a ladder, and a bucket of water and you've got an *I Love Lucy* episode waiting to happen. Even prepasted wallpaper rolls are hard to manage, because it's the first law of physics that an 8-foot-long piece of paper will stick to me before it sticks to the wall.

That's why I love working with pieces of paper or mat board and adhering them to the wall like tiles. This idea is apparently catching on, because now manufacturers are making paper tiles. I absolutely flipped when I found these three-dimensional ones, called V2 wallpaper tiles. Shapes extend out of the tile, so when several are placed together, they create unique wallscapes. And depending on the time of day and how the light is shining, the look changes. Standing back, the wall looks like gentle sand dunes. Closer up, the shapes look like computer-generated topography, or microscopic spores. I also love that these V2 tiles are eco-friendly, made from 100 percent post- and pre-consumer waste paper.

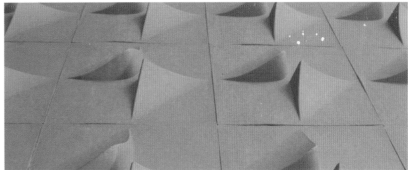

WHERE TO BUY IT

V2 tiles are available directly from the manufacturer, which I've listed in the Resource Directory. You can purchase the 3M Command Picture Hanging Strips at hardware and picture frame stores.

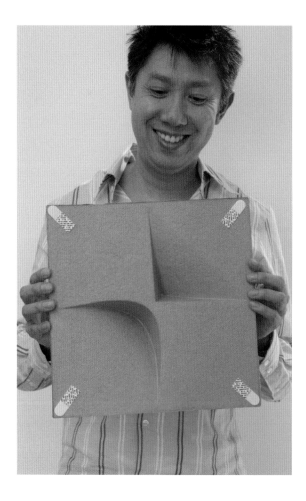

1 PLACE ADHESIVE STRIPS ON THE TILES

On the back of every tile, put a 3M Command Picture Hanging Strip on each corner. These adhesive strips are ideal because they come off without damaging your wall. If you can't find the 3M strips, you can also use double-stick tape or museum putty (I use The Museum Putty™ or Quake Hold!™). Of course, you can also use a more permanent paste adhesive, but the strips will hold the tiles as long as you want them while still giving you the option of removing them later.

2 PLACE THE TILES ON THE WALL

Taking your first paper tile, use a laser level to make sure the tile is lined up straight (see page 41 for instructions on how to use a laser level). Then press the tile at the adhesion point for thirty seconds. Because you presumably have only two hands, press on the top two corners first and then the bottom two corners.

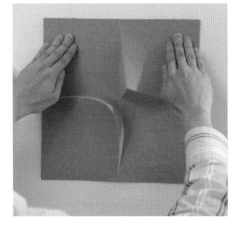

HELPFUL HINT

The 3M strips have a section that's sticky and one that's not. Position the sticky section of the strip toward the center of the tile rather than toward the corner. It's important to do it this way because there is a slight rim at the corners of the tiles, and the adhesive would not have direct contact with the wall at that point. Having the adhesive section positioned toward the inside of the tile will help keep the tile in place.

Next, start applying the tiles consecutively. The straight edges will help you line them up easily. Every now and then, use the level to make sure you're lining them up straight.

Besides being simple to install, these wall tiles are a breeze to remove. You can reuse them; and when you're through with them, they're recyclable. This wall treatment also looks great when it doesn't cover the entire wall. As a freestanding square or rectangle on the wall, it doubles as a piece of art.

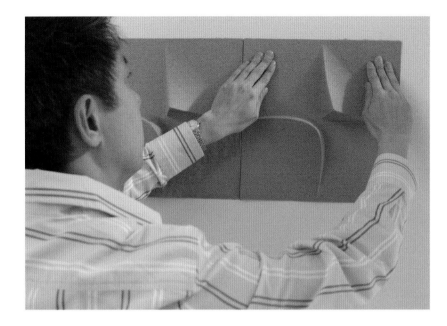

KEEPING IT CLEAN

Occasionally dust the tiles, and this wall treatment will always look like new. Like many of the projects in this book, you can remove any sections that need to be replaced and put up new ones, so keep a supply of extra tiles just in case.

ANOTHER IDEA

You can also make your own tiles. At many art supply stores, you can find sheets of decorating paper that have the most unusual textures like those shown in the photograph below. People buy them for art projects; but cut down to squares, they work beautifully on a wall. You can even mix and match papers. These decorative papers are usually around 20 x 26 inches. They can be paper thin or, more typically, have the thickness of poster board. Using an X-Acto knife, cut each sheet on a cutting mat horizontally and vertically into four squares of 10 x 10 inches. You'll have a small piece left over that you can save for other projects. Then attach these tiles to the wall with the same adhesive strips.

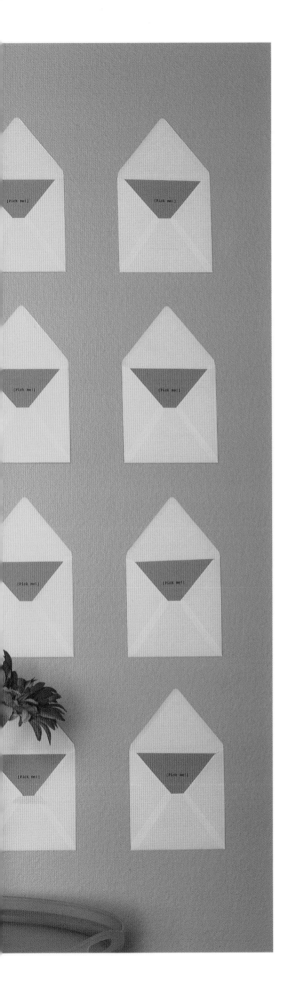

Chapter 14

The Envelope, Please: A Grid of Envelopes Wins an Award for Creativity

LEVEL OF EASE: ③

ETW (ESTIMATED TIME OF WOW): 4 hours

RECOMMENDED MUSIC: Vanessa Williams. *Sweetest Days*

Maybe it's because I grew up in a Chinese restaurant, but I love fortune cookies. Well, not the cookies themselves exactly, but the fortunes inside them. There's that magical moment right before you break open the cookie when you feel in your bones that this fortune is special. It was written just for you. And yes, this fortune will come true. Especially when you add "in bed" to the end of it.

Fortunes are the inspiration behind this colorful wall treatment. Fun prophecies or affirmations are written on note cards, which are tucked away in coordinating envelopes. How wonderful it is to have a wall that gives you an affirmation whenever you need a little lift. It will be the first place that guests go when they enter your house. And you can refresh the messages whenever you feel like it, or adjust them according to the season or occasion. This would also make a great wall treatment for a party. I predict fun will be had by all.

1 DECIDE ON A LAYOUT

First, decide how you'd like to configure the envelopes on your wall. Of course, it depends on the size of your envelopes, but on a typical 8-foot wall with 6-x-6-inch envelopes, I find that four horizontal rows of envelopes work best. If you go too high, you can't reach the upper row; and if you go too low, you're constantly running into them with your grocery bags. How many vertical rows you have will depend on how wide your wall is. On a 10-foot-wide wall, about seven or eight rows will be sufficient.

2 PLACE HORIZONTAL LINES

Now let's start mapping out the location of the envelopes. Using a laser level (see page 41), indicate a horizontal straight line that's around eye level. (Your eye level, not Shaquille O'Neal's.) Take a piece of masking tape and line it up with the laser line.

Then start adding parallel pieces of masking tape that are equidistant apart above and below this first piece, also using the laser level. Stand back and eyeball the lines to make sure they look evenly spaced. Keep in mind that you don't want the envelopes higher than a person can reach, so I wouldn't recommend more than two rows above the one at eye level.

3 PLACE VERTICAL LINES

Next, use the laser level to indicate the vertical lines. Start with where you want the middle row of envelopes to go. After lining up the masking tape to this laser line, repeat and add masking tape to the left and right of the middle line, at equal distances apart. When you're done, you should have a lovely masking tape grid.

4 SPRAY ADHESIVE ONTO THE ENVELOPES

Go outside and spray the front side of each envelope with an adhesive, working over some old newspapers or a large piece of cardboard. The adhesive spray gets everywhere, so I don't recommend doing it indoors. You're spraying the front of the envelope because the back is what will be facing out. To save time, you can spray several envelopes at once before attaching them. In fact, the adhesive becomes even stickier when you allow time for it to settle. If you're planning a temporary version of this wall treatment, apply a dab of museum putty to the five corners of each envelope instead. When you want to take down the envelopes, the putty comes right off (see page 75 for instructions on how to remove putty from walls).

5 PRESS ENVELOPES ONTO THE WALL

Line up the bottom left corner of the envelope with the bottom left corner of the masking tape grid and press the envelope onto the wall so the adhesive holds. Repeat for all envelopes, and when you're finished, remove the masking tape. Now you're ready to fill the envelopes with fortunes.

6 WRITE YOUR FORTUNES

Use your imagination and write a number of fortunes or affirmations on each note card, or type them using a word processing program and print them out on each card. If you didn't grow up in a Chinese restaurant and have trouble coming up with wise proverbs, look through your local newspaper's horoscope for ideas. Have fun with them. You can even tailor the fortunes to specific people who you know will be reading them. Then place one note card in each envelope.

KEEPING IT CLEAN

The interactive nature of this wall treatment means that people will be taking the note cards in and out of envelopes constantly, so both cards and envelopes will get a lot of wear and tear. If they become wrinkled or full of fingerprints, it's time for new ones.

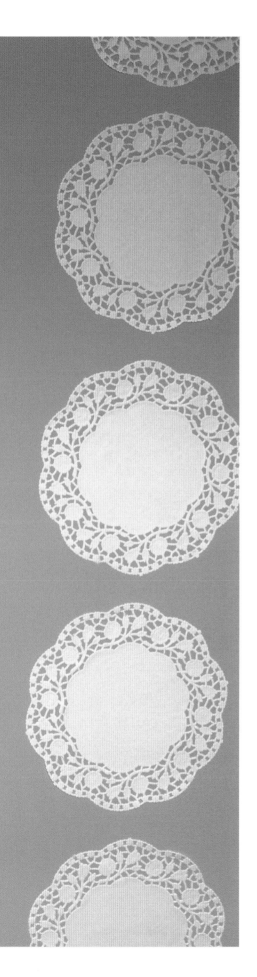

Chapter 15

Hello Doily: Shabby Chic that's Deliciously Easy

LEVEL OF EASE: 2

ETW (ESTIMATED TIME OF WOW): 2 hours

RECOMMENDED MUSIC: Herb Alpert. *Whipped Cream & Other Delights*

I've never given paper doilies a second look. Like most people, I've always been more concerned with what chocolate goody was on top of it. It was as utilitarian as a napkin, and maybe even less so. But one day, I took a closer look and appreciated the intricate beauty of this carved-out piece of paper, as lovely as a snowflake, and knew immediately that it would be the basis of a charming wall project.

This elegant wall treatment conjures up memories of high tea with my aunt, cotillion balls, and cricket matches. Not that I've ever been to any of those things, but I do have a vivid imagination. You have to admit, though, that this look is wonderfully evocative of a more refined era. And the fact that it's created with paper doilies gives it a sense of humor, so it's not snobby in the least.

WHERE TO BUY IT

Never having bought paper doilies before, I thought they might be hard to find. But I needn't have worried, because they were everywhere! Who knew? You can get them at grocery stores, home stores, restaurant supply stores, party stores, and online. They also come in different widths, shapes, designs, and colors.

1 TAPE A VERTICAL LINE

We'll be creating vertical rows of doilies, so we need to create a template with masking tape to help us place them on the wall in a straight line. Using a laser level to guide you, create the first vertical line with the masking tape, going straight up and down from about the ceiling to the floor (see page 41 for instructions on how to use a laser level). Now there's one question I'm sure you're asking at this point: what on earth is going on with my hair in these photos?

2 SPACE THE OTHER VERTICAL LINES

Again using a laser level, place your second vertical piece of masking tape 21-1/2 inches away from the first. Why that distance? It is the approximate width of two doilies placed side by side. To make sure you've spaced them correctly, hold up two doilies to double check. Create as many vertical lines as you want to fill your wall.

3 TAPE A HORIZONTAL LINE

Next, using the laser level, place a horizontal strip of masking tape on the wall. Just make it as wide as you want the wall treatment to be. There will be room for about six doilies in each vertical row, so you will be putting up six horizontal lines of masking tape in this template.

4 SPACE THE OTHER HORIZONTAL LINES

You'll be spacing the horizontal lines of masking tape so that one doily fits within two lines. Hold up a doily between the masking tape to make sure the lines are evenly spaced.

5 FINISH THE MASKING TAPE GRID

Keep going till you've created a grid template on the wall; you will now know exactly where to place each doily. Let's move on to the doilies.

6 SEPARATE THE DOILIES

The doilies are stuck together very tightly in their package, so carefully separate the doilies from each other. This seems like such an obvious step; but believe me, as I was putting doilies on the wall, I found a few times when I hadn't properly separated them, and I was placing two on the wall instead of one.

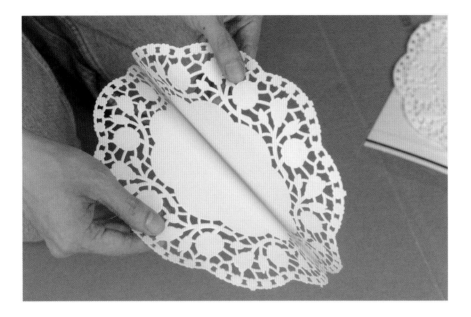

7 SPRAY THE BACK OF EACH DOILY WITH ADHESIVE

Go outside and place about four doilies on a large piece of cardboard or news papers. Spray each doily with an even coat of 3M Super 77 Spray Adhesive, pointing the nozzle at a 90-degree angle from the doilies. (If you spray at a shallower angle, the spray might cause the doilies to fly up.) Then carefully bring the sticky doilies inside. It might help to have someone assist you bring them in.

8 PLACE THE DOILIES ON THE WALL

Place the doily between the masking tape lines and roll a rubber brayer over the doily. The brayer presses the doily securely to the wall without ripping the delicate details in the paper. Using your bare hands does not work as effectively.

HELPFUL HINT

Many doilies, like the ones pictured in this project, have scalloped edges. When lining up the doilies against the masking tape, be consistent with where you're placing the scalloped edge. For example, in the photograph to the left, you can see I've attached the doily to the wall with one edge touching the horizontal masking tape and two scalloped edges touching the vertical piece.

9 REMOVE THE MASKING TAPE

My favorite part. After you've completed each row, remove the masking tape to survey your work. The final result will be wonderfully repeating rows of pearly white doilies, as in the photograph below. If you're having a tea party, be sure to invite me.

KEEPING IT CLEAN

Frankly, it's easier to replace any doilies that get dirty than to clean them. Just peel off the old doily with your fingers and replace it with a fresh one. So be sure to keep a package of new doilies handy in case you need them.

Part V:
Ideas that Stick

One reason many people don't do anything with their walls is that they're afraid of committing to a color or a style. What happens if they don't like it? What happens if they get tired of it? Once it's on the wall, it's permanent, isn't it? Not at all. For all of you afraid of long-term commitments, here are the wall treatments for you—the design elements adhere to the wall, but they can be easily removed. These are the one-night stands of walls. The "Not Mr. Right, but Mr. Right Now" walls. The "Love Me and Leave Me" walls. The . . . well, you get the idea.

Chapter 16

Cute As a Button: Vintage Buttons Add Charm and Cheer

LEVEL OF EASE: 2

ETW (ESTIMATED TIME OF WOW): 6 hours

RECOMMENDED MUSIC: Go-Go's. *Beauty and the Beat*

When I design a teenager's room, I'm frequently asked to come up with a design that appeals to the teen now (as in this week) but can be changed easily when he or she grows out of it (like next week). The room shown, which was designed for a thirteen-year-old, combines the fun that the girl wanted with a more grown-up sensibility I knew would come once she got older. But the decor still had to be easily changed, since she would undoubtedly change her tastes in the years to come.

What's my secret weapon for quick-and-easy change-outs? My old favorite, museum putty. It attaches lightweight objects to the wall really well, and it comes off just like that. For this wall, I arranged buttons in diamond patterns and alternated the rows with coordinating ribbons. People who see the buttons assume they've been attached with glue or epoxy, but it's just museum putty. Boy, I should buy stock in it.

WHERE TO BUY IT

For this wall treatment you need lots of buttons. You can buy them in quantity for very little money at a weekend flea market, which is where I got the buttons for this wall. A whole bag of several hundred cost me $9. You can also check eBay® for used buttons. The key is to get a variety. Also, try not to get shank buttons. The shanks jut out, making it hard to adhere them to the wall. Instead, get ones with buttonholes.

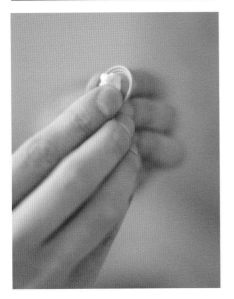

1 PUT SOME PUTTY ON THE BUTTONS

Take a small dab of putty and place it on the back of the button. Don't put on so much putty that it oozes out the sides, but do put on enough so the button will hold.

OTHER IDEAS

Besides buttons, you can attach other lightweight objects with museum putty. For example, guitar picks come in many colors and look great in a music room. And plastic cutlery is pretty amusing flying all over the walls in a kitchen or breakfast nook.

2 ARRANGE THE BUTTONS IN A DIAMOND SHAPE

When making the diamonds, select buttons that are of the same color family, so that each diamond has its distinct look. In the diamond in the photo, I've chosen buttons in the green color family, which includes olives, mint, and Kelly—all shades of green. Another color family might be golds, oranges, and yellows, which have a common hue. They shouldn't be the identical type of button; in fact, you should vary the sizes. But using buttons in the same color family makes each diamond a cohesive whole.

Trying to randomly form a diamond shape will result in something pretty assymetrical, so start by placing the top button of the diamond, then the bottom, then the left, then the right. After the four points of the diamond are placed, you can fill in the middle points.

3 PLACE A RIBBON BETWEEN THE DIAMONDS

After you've completed a vertical row of diamonds, add a ribbon going from the ceiling to the floor. This sets off the row, so your eye sees diamonds rather than a mishmash of buttons. Stretch the ribbon taut, and staple the ribbon at the top and bottom.

Cover the unsightly staple on the ribbon with a large button, and put nails through two of the buttonholes to secure it.

HELPFUL HINT

Keep some extra museum putty on hand in case you bump into the wall and dislodge some of the buttons during a rambunctious pillow fight. Also, if you have a cat that will eat the buttons off the wall, I wouldn't recommend this wall treatment—unless you use kitty treats instead of buttons for the diamonds. And of course, if there are babies or small children around, you shouldn't do this wall treatment unless the buttons are out of their reach.

4 DO TWO ROWS AT A TIME

If you alternate one or two rows of buttons with some blank wall space (as in the photograph below), the wall will look less busy and you will be able to incorporate shelving and other furniture without drowning them in buttons.

KEEPING IT CLEAN

Dust the buttons gently with a feather duster every so often. Be careful, because if you're too vigorous with the duster, you'll knock the buttons off the wall.

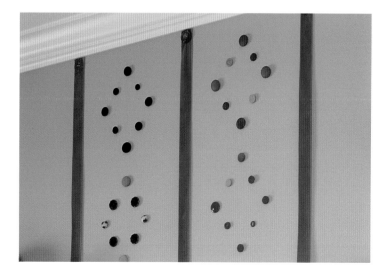

Believe in peace, fairness and chocolate chip cookie

Subliminal messages I will buy more copies of this book are a myth.

Kindness is a language that the deaf can h

The best things in life aren't things.

Never trust

If you want to find a s

No rain, no rainbow.

sift throug

When all else fails, do your happy dance.

Follow your heart and you'll

If it weren't for the last minute, nothing would get done.

Chapter 17

If Walls Could Speak: Favorite Quotes Will Have Everyone Talking

> **LEVEL OF EASE:** 2
>
> **ETW (ESTIMATED TIME OF WOW):** 3 hours
>
> **RECOMMENDED MUSIC:** Rufus Wainwright. *Poses*

I'm sure you've heard the old saying, "A picture is worth a thousand words." Well, when it comes to walls, a word can be worth a thousand pictures. That's right, who needs pictures when you have words? Words can be stunning on a wall, and they're a great way to personalize your space. Imagine your favorite poem in your living room, a collection of inspirational affirmations in your office, or a nursery rhyme in a child's bedroom. The possibilities are endless.

For years, I had gone to museums, admiring not just the artwork, but the verbiage on the walls that explained the pieces. While patrons were studying the intricacies of Pointillism and Impressionism, I was looking at the paragraphs on the wall, asking myself, "How did they put up those words? Are they stencils or rub-ons? How can I do that in someone's house?" Yes, I'm strange that way.

After doing a little research, I found that these words are vinyl letters that are insanely easy to rub onto your walls. And they're not just easy, they're addictive. When I've had novices help me apply the vinyl words, they became experts in a matter of minutes, and they didn't want to stop. So put the whole family to work. They'll love it.

WHERE TO BUY IT

You can order your custom words at a sign shop because they are the same vinyl letters used by businesses to apply copy to their windows. However, I've found that it's easier just to order them over the Internet. There are several great companies (included in the Resource Directory) that specialize in producing these vinyl words for home decorators just like you.

1 DECIDE WHAT YOU'RE GOING TO SAY

The creative part of this wall treatment is figuring out what you're going to say on the walls. Besides a favorite poem or affirmations, consider using famous quotes from movies, your wedding vows, Bible verses, jokes, absolutely anything that reflects your personality.

2 PICK COLORS, SIZES, AND FONTS

Vinyl letters come in a rainbow of colors, every font imaginable, and sizes from 1/2-inch letters on up to 12 inches or more. I recommend at least two colors, so there is more visual interest. A mixture of small and large letters has more impact. Don't go font crazy, however. I wouldn't choose more than two different fonts or the effect starts looking messy. In the wall pictured here, I've chosen one font in two colors and in various sizes.

3 ARRANGE YOUR WORDS ON THE WALL

Your words will come to you prespaced and lined up in sentences. The vinyl words are sandwiched in between two layers. The top layer is the transfer paper you'll be rubbing to apply the letters, and the bottom layer is the protective backing you'll peel off and discard before rubbing the letters. Keep all the layers together. No peeling, please, as tempting as it may be at this point.

First, use masking tape to attach all the sentences to the wall. At this early stage, don't worry if they're straight. Just keep arranging the sentences until you're happy with the general placement. Have fun with this part. You can make sentences wrap around walls, read vertically, or outline a window.

Once the sentences are where you want them, use a laser level to line up the bottoms of the letters and readjust the masking tape accordingly (see page 41 for instructions on how to use a laser level).

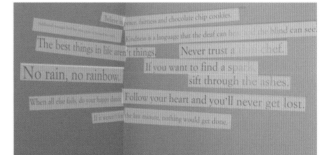

Using a wooden craft stick, rub the letters with all the layers intact. Why are you doing this? The vinyl letters were originally created on the bottom protective backing layer. Now we want these letters to stick to the top transfer layer instead. Rubbing the layers with a stick will make this happen.

With the masking tape acting as a hinge, lift the sheet and peel off the backing paper. It should come right off, but every now and then the letters remain stuck to it. When that happens, just rub the top layer with the stick some more, and the letter will separate from the backing layer.

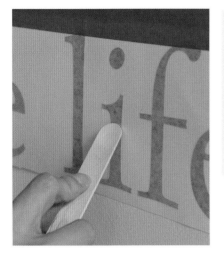

HELPFUL HINT

Once the words are arranged on the wall, cut the sentences up into manageable 1-foot sections. This will make peeling off the backing paper a lot easier.

6 RUB THE TOP LAYER DIRECTLY ONTO THE WALL

Now all that should remain is the top layer, which you'll notice is sticky, and the actual vinyl letters. Press the sheet onto the wall so it stays in place and start rubbing the vinyl letters through the top transfer layer.

When you've finished, slowly peel off the top layer. The vinyl letters will remain on the wall. As you're peeling, some letters will occasionally stick to the top layer and not stay on the wall. In fact, count on it. Just take your stick and rub the letters down some more, and they will eventually adhere to the wall. Every now and then, stand back and survey your work. There's something exhilarating about the "reveal" moment in this process when you've peeled off the top layer and see the words that you've applied.

REMOVING THE WORDS

When you move or redecorate, it's easy to remove all the words. Use an X-Acto® knife to turn up the edges of the letters and peel them off with your fingernails. Warming up the letters with a hair dryer makes it even easier.

KEEPING IT CLEAN

Because the words are made of vinyl, they are so easy to clean with a damp cloth. But, really, you shouldn't be squirting ketchup at them anyway.

Chapter 18

Different Stripes: Paper Tape for an Instant Rainbow of Colors

> **LEVEL OF EASE:** ①
>
> **ETW (ESTIMATED TIME OF WOW):** 1-1/2 hours
>
> **RECOMMENDED MUSIC:** Pink Floyd. *Dark Side of the Moon*

I love the look of stripes on a wall. They're both retro and contemporary, like a Doris Day movie crossed with a *Desperate Housewives* episode. And those vertical lines are so slimming. But painting stripes can be a hassle, because even when you use masking tape it's hard to get perfectly straight lines. There is a secret, however, and it's in the masking tape.

This is not your father's masking tape, though. It's actually paper tape, called Permacel®, that comes in a variety of colors, like bright red and orange, lime green, baby blue, and royal purple. And they come in various widths, from razor thin to superwide. So instead of putting up masking tape, painting around it, and removing the tape, you put up stripes of different-colored tape and leave them.

This wall treatment is so easy, it's almost embarrassing to include it in this book. But that's precisely why I've included it. When ideas are this simple, we think they couldn't possibly be good. But difficulty does not equate with style. It's this wall's utter simplicity that contributes to its "WOW" factor.

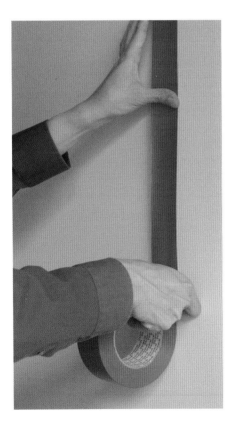

1 CHOOSE YOUR COLOR SCHEME

Before applying the tape, it's a good idea to paint your wall with a
base color that's distinct from the stripe colors. That way, the wall
color will act as another stripe. Then you can select tape colors that
will complement the wall color. For the yellow wall in this demonstration, I chose red, orange, and light blue because I loved the
happy combination of those colors.

2 READY, SET, TAPE

Using your laser level to guide you, apply your first color of tape
vertically to the wall (see page 41 for instructions on how to use a
laser level). Start the tape about an inch above the top of the wall.
Slowly unrolling the tape, lightly press the tape every few inches
along the laser line to hold it temporarily. When you're
satisfied that the entire stripe is straight, tear the tape about an
inch below the bottom of the wall and press the entire length
firmly with your fingertips to adhere it.

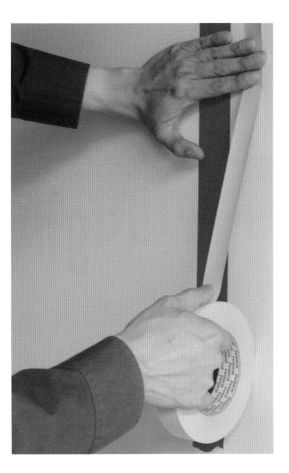

3 KEEP GOING

For your next stripe, choose a different color and a different width. Using your laser level, indicate a line to the right of the first stripe where you will be placing the new stripe. If you place it close to the first stripe, you will create a thin stripe comprising the base wall color. If you place it farther away, you will create a larger stripe of the wall color. As you apply subsequent stripes, keep varying your pattern. You can repeat colors and widths, too. There is no right or wrong way to do it.

CLOSE ENOUGH

After each stripe is applied, step back to appreciate the effect and make sure everything's straight. If a particular stripe appears crooked or if you decide you don't want that color there, just take it off and start over. You'll have more tape than you need to complete this wall, so experiment.

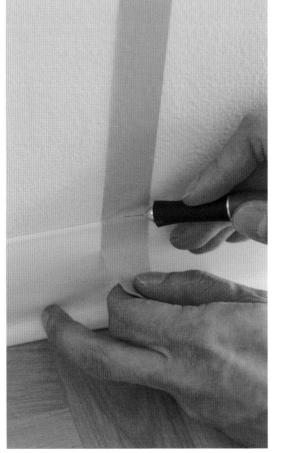

4 TRIM THE EDGES

At the top and bottom of the wall where you've torn the tape, take an X-Acto knife and trim the tape so it's flush with the ceiling or floor molding. Now, step back and survey your masterpiece. Looking at it, no one would believe that it's just masking tape. Go ahead, let people think you painstakingly painted each stripe. It will be our little secret.

REMOVING THE TAPE

When you want to change the look, the tape peels right off. You can even remove an entire section of stripes and replace them with all-new colors.

KEEPING IT CLEAN

Use a damp cloth, but rub it in an up-and-down motion, in the direction of the tape. This way, you won't accidentally lift the tape off at the sides.

Chapter 19

Poetry in Motion: Ever-Changing Verse on a Magnetic Wall

LEVEL OF EASE: ③

ETW (ESTIMATED TIME OF WOW): 7 hours
(plus paint drying time)

RECOMMENDED MUSIC: Amy Grant. *Behind the Eyes*

Poetic words will float on air.
Held by magnets you can't tell are there.
It's a wall that's sure to wow.
Follow closely, and I'll show you how.

All right, I'm not the best poet. But here's an idea that makes creating poetry fun and easy. Similar to the magnetic words seen on many of today's finest refrigerators, this wall treatment allows you to make your own poetry on a grander scale. By moving words around, you can create phrases that are sometimes humorous, often clever, and accidentally deep. And because the words are movable, you can interchange them whenever you want. Everyone who walks into your house will shuffle the words around in some way. They can't help it.

But how do the words stay put? The magic is in the hidden coat of magnetic paint applied to the wall underneath the regular wall color. No one will even know it's there. *So you'll be certain to amaze, With an ever-changing phrase.* Okay, I'll stop now.

WHERE TO BUY IT

Some paint stores carry magnetic paint, but they often only carry the small pint size, which doesn't cover much surface area. I ordered it directly from the manufacturer's Web site, which is listed in the Resource Directory. See page 16 for information on buying foam core.

HELPFUL HINT

Be sure to stir the magnetic paint really well so that the metallic particles are evenly distributed. Even as you're applying the coats, keep stirring the paint. Otherwise, there might not be enough metal on the walls to attract magnets.

1 MAGNETIZE YOUR WALL

Use masking tape to section off the part of the wall that you will be magnetizing. It's not essential to do this step, as the entire wall will be covered by regular paint anyway, but I like to be neat and orderly. Something to do with my childhood, I'm sure. Then paint three coats of the magnetic paint onto the wall. Although the paint is called magnetic, it's technically not magnetic at all. Instead, the paint is full of metallic particles, which allow magnets to adhere to it. So don't worry that you've created a huge magnetic force that will cause household appliances and children wearing braces to fly across the room. After you've painted three coats, paint over the magnetic paint with the wall's regular color.

2 CHOOSE YOUR WORDS

For your poetry, words like *love, trust, me, you, patience, never, want,* and *eyes* work really well. After all, what love song doesn't have those words in them? But it's also fun to mix it up a little with totally random ones like *kangaroo, television,* and *bodacious.* (And let's keep it clean, folks.) It's a good idea to create more words than you are planning on putting on the wall, so you have a backup supply.

Then, input each word into a word processor or a graphics program. Change the typeface for each word and, if you have a color printer, change the color as well. Print the words on an 8-1/2-x-11-inch piece of paper (or 11-x-17-inch if you have a larger printer).

3 MOUNT YOUR WORDS

Spray a layer of adhesive on the back of each sheet of paper and mount the pieces to the foam core. (When using a spray adhesive, I recommend using it outside and placing a large piece of cardboard or old newspapers under whatever you're spraying.) Then trim them with an X-Acto knife on a cutting mat. Using a straightedge will help you get an even cut. Now, I may not be wearing protective gloves in the photograph, but I do recommend that you do.

4 ADD STRIPS OF MAGNETIC TAPE

Finally, place two strips of magnetic tape on the back of the foam core. Long strips work better than dots or squares because the more surface area of magnetic material there is, the better the foam core stays on the wall. Now you can start making poetry.

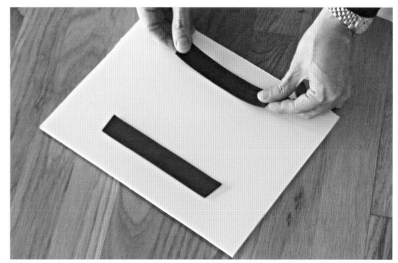

OTHER IDEAS

Once your wall is magnetized, you don't have to be limited to poetry. Instead of words, you can use pictures of different heads, torsos, and legs to make mix-and-match people. Or create a wall-sized tic-tac-toe game. You can constantly change the look.

KEEPING IT CLEAN

Everyone will be moving these words around frequently, so the boards will get fingerprints and even dents. When the words looks like they've seen better days, put them out of their misery. Just make new words. Besides, it'll keep your poetry skills fresh.

Chapter 20

Into the Woods: The Easiest Wood Paneling in the World

> **LEVEL OF EASE:** ⑤
>
> **ETW (ESTIMATED TIME OF WOW):** 5 hours
>
> (with lots of waiting time in between)
>
> **RECOMMENDED MUSIC:** The Carpenters. *Gold: 35th Anniversary Edition*

Wood paneling has a natural warmth and richness that makes you feel instantly comfortable and at home. No wonder it's been a favorite wall covering for centuries. But maneuvering those 8-foot planks in a lumberyard can be ultra-intimidating, especially with the sound of buzz saws in the air. And once you get them home, that's another installation nightmare.

Well, I've got a solution that will give you all the beauty of real wood without the hard work. The secret is balsa wood. It's an extremely lightweight wood typically used for making model airplanes. Balsa stains beautifully in rich colors yet is as easy to work with as poster board. And it's so light, it attaches to the wall with double-stick tape! You've got to love that.

In this project, I've created a craftsman look by varying the sizes and colors of the wood panels. The look is simultaneously masculine and elegant, like me—if I were Cary Grant. It would look great across an entire wall or in a small section for, say, a headboard.

Balsa wood sheets, 1/32-inch
  thickness in various sizes
Cutting mat
Double-stick mounting tape
Drop cloth or plastic sheet
5 all-purpose paintbrushes,
  3 inches wide
General-purpose leather
  work gloves
Laser level
Pencil
Rubber gloves
Straightedge
Steel wool (grade "000")
Tack cloth
Wood conditioner
Wood stain and sealer in one,
  4 shades
X-Acto® knife

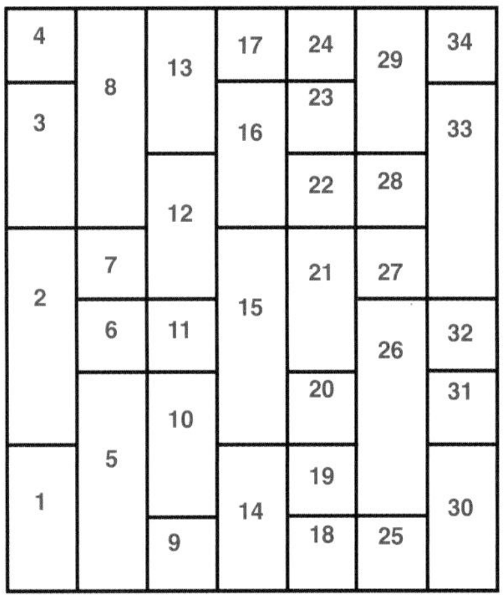

WHERE TO BUY IT

Balsa wood is available in arts and crafts stores, as well as model airplane shops. However, what you'll typically find at these retailers is narrower pieces of wood, usually not more than 3 inches wide. To find the 1-foot widths, I went online and bought directly from balsa wood manufacturers. I've listed some Web sites in the Resource Directory, and it takes about two weeks for the shipment to arrive. The sheets are available in sizes ranging from 1-x-2 feet to 1-x-4 feet, but I don't recommend using the 4-foot length because the wood has a tendency to warp when it's that large. And remember to purchase one sheet of 1-x-2-foot balsa wood for every two 1-x-1-foot sheets in your diagram. A quick note about that huge supply list: I know that I always avoid recipes that require too many ingredients, but don't be put off by all the materials needed here. I've recommended them to make your job easier, and they can all be found in one or two aisles at the hardware store.

1 CREATE A DIAGRAM

The first step is to create a diagram, and to do that you have to decide what size panels you want to use and how much wall space you want to cover. Since my wall is 8 feet high, I diagrammed a 7-x-8-foot expanse of wood. Decide if you want to use the two easy-to-work-with sizes that balsa wood comes in—1-x-2 feet and 1-x-3 feet—or if you want to work with a third size (which is accomplished by cutting the 1-x-2-foot sheets in half; we'll get to that later). Since I like the visual variety, I used three sizes of balsa in this project: 1-x-1 feet, 1-x-2 feet, and 1-x-3 feet. Once you've decided which sizes of balsa wood panels you'd like to use, you're ready to map out how you want the different-sized panels to lay on the wall. I drew my schematic diagram using a computer program, but you can do it by hand as well. Next, number each box in the diagram, going from bottom to top; you'll use these numbers as a reference later. The total number of boxes also tells you how many panels you should buy. (Get a few extra, just in case.)

2 TRIM THE WOOD, IF NECESSARY

To make 1-x-1-foot pieces, 1-x-2-foot pieces need to be cut in half. Now, the thought of sawing wood in a straight line sends shivers through my body. But the great thing about balsa wood is that you can just cut it with an X-Acto knife, especially since we're working with the 1/32-inch thickness. Place the panel on a cutting mat, line up the straight edge, and slice. The balsa wood is so thin, it cuts without any effort. For extra safety, wear a glove on the hand holding the straightedge.

3 NUMBER EACH PANEL TO CORRESPOND TO THE DIAGRAM

On the back of each piece of wood, write the number that corresponds to the number you've assigned it in the diagram. This way you'll know how the pieces fit together on the wall, even if the panels get separated.

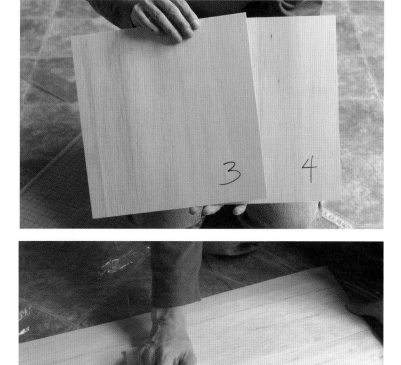

4 WIPE DUST OFF THE WOOD

Now place a drop cloth (or plastic sheet) on the floor, because the fun is about to start. Using a tack cloth, wipe each piece of wood to remove all dust. If you've never used one before, a tack cloth is a sticky cloth that you'll find in the paint department of the hardware store. It's a wonderful invention.

5 APPLY WOOD CONDITIONER TO EACH PANEL

Because balsa wood is so soft, it doesn't accept wood stain as easily and evenly as hard woods do. But applying a coat of wood conditioner (like Minwax® Pre-Stain Wood Conditioner) solves this problem. Using a 3-inch brush, paint the conditioner on each balsa panel. It absorbs instantaneously and dries in less than fifteen minutes. You may be tempted to skip this step. How much of a difference does the conditioner make, after all? Trust me, it makes a huge difference. Without it, your stain will go on blotchy, and you may end up using more stain in the long run to cover the uneven spots.

6 ASSIGN STAIN COLORS TO EACH PANEL

On the same schematic diagram that you've already created, assign stain colors to each panel so you can plan ahead how you're distributing the various colors. I've used four different stain colors to create a beautiful montage of woods: honey pine, pecan, Bombay mahogany, and natural cherry, all in a satin finish. I recommend using a product that combines stain and polyurethane in one, like Minwax PolyShades®, so you don't need to apply a sealer in a separate step. As you can see in the diagram, I've alternated the colors so that panels of the same color do not touch, but it's perfectly all right to have like-colored panels meet, as it would create some interesting L- and T-shaped patterns.

4 cherry		13 cherry	17 pine	24 mahog	29 cherry	34 pine
	8 mahog			23 pine		33
3 pecan			16			
		12 pine		pecan	22 cherry	28 pine	pecan
2 pine	7 cherry		15 mahog	21 pecan	mahog 27	32 cherry
	6 mahog	11 pecan			26 pine	31 mahog
		10 cherry		20 cherry		
1 mahog	5 pecan		14 pecan	19 pine		30 pecan
		9 pine		18 mahog	25 cherry	

7 APPLY TWO COATS OF STAIN AND SEALER

Put on your rubber gloves, open your four cans of stain, and brush on a coat of color using the diagram as your guide. Assemble all the panels that correspond to a particular finish and stain those at the same time. For example, you know that panels 4, 7, 10, and 13 are to be stained in the natural cherry finish, so do those together. After one coat, the wood already looks glorious, but it will take a second coat to give each panel a satin glow. Wait at least six hours for the first coat to dry completely. Then apply the second coat and wait another six hours for that coat to dry. Obviously, you'll want to work in a ventilated garage or carport. Give yourself plenty of room to spread out, and be careful on those knees.

8 POLISH WITH STEEL WOOL

At this point, you'll be marveling at how beautiful your wood panels are, and you'll be anxious to put them on the wall. But first, buff each panel with an extra-fine grade of steel wool (grade "ooo" or higher) to smooth out any uneven sections. If it looks like the finish is uniform throughout, you can skip this step. (Wow, you're good.)

9 PUT DOUBLE-STICK TAPE ON THE BACK

I just love that these wood panels are attached to the wall with double-stick mounting tape. It takes away all the intimidation of installing wood paneling. On the back of each piece of wood, place a strip of tape on the left and right sides. In the photo to the right, you can see that I've used a strip of tape that runs the whole length of the wood. Is this much tape necessary? Not always. If a particular panel happens to be warped, a long piece of tape will help keep it from jutting out from the wall. But if the panel lies flat, all you will actually need is a 1-inch piece on each corner, plus a 1-inch piece on each of the sides.

ANOTHER APPROACH

Staining all the panels in color groups as I've suggested is a simpler method in terms of organization. But here's another approach that lets you see how the different panels will actually be arranged on the wall. It requires more working space and a big drop cloth. Position the panels on the floor in the exact arrangement as your diagram, leaving some room between each of the panels so you can walk around them. Then stain them as they're laid out. This way, as you're working, you'll get a better idea of how the colors will juxtapose with one another.

10 STICK THE WOOD TO THE WALL

Starting at the bottom, tuck your first wood panel between the molding and the wall if there is a big enough gap to squeeze it in, and press the panel where the double-stick tape touches the wall. If it won't fit behind the molding, just place the bottom edge of the panel flush up against the top edge of the molding. Make sure you use a laser level to line up the panel straight (see page 41 for instructions on how to use a laser level).

HELPFUL HINT

If you need to remove any of the wood panels, be very careful because the balsa wood is so thin. If you pull it away from the wall, the wood will crack. Instead, take a long putty knife and wedge it underneath the wood and double-stick tape to pry it loose. You should do this if you ever take down the entire wall treatment so you can save the panels to reuse elsewhere.

11 INSTALL ONE ROW AT A TIME

Then start moving up the row. Why do I go from bottom to top? There's a method to my madness. After the bottom panel is attached, you can use it as a guide by resting the next one on top of it and then pressing down on the double-stick tape. After you've finished one row, go to the next row and start at the bottom again, and use your laser level to make sure you're not veering off at an angle. You'll get into a good rhythm here, especially if you have someone help you peel the double-stick tape. You'll find that the prep work for this wall is the most time-consuming part of it; putting it up takes just minutes.

KEEPING IT CLEAN

Nothing maintains this wall treatment better than a tack cloth. Keep your cloth in the plastic wrapper so it remains sticky, and periodically wipe the wood with it. For tougher stains, a damp cloth will clean the wood without harming it, since you've sealed the wood with polyurethane.

CLOSE ENOUGH

The balsa wood sheets come from the manufacturer with straight edges, but even so, as you're lining them up against one another, they may not be completely flush. Don't stress out about it. If your wall is a dark color, you won't even see the gaps. Another thing you can do is overlap the panels to get rid of the gaps. The wood is thin enough so that you'll hardly notice the overlap.

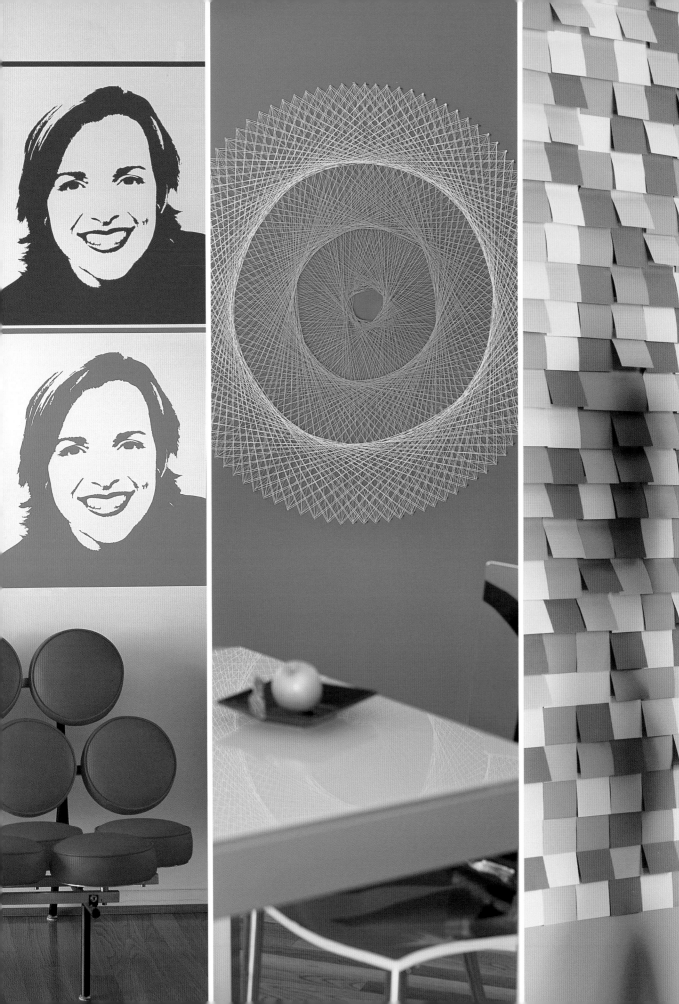

Part VI:
Your Wall As Art

Michelangelo turned a ceiling into a work of art. I want to help you do the same to a wall. Think of your wall as an empty canvas waiting to unleash your creative spirit. I can imagine the next wall treatments in any Modern Art museum, surrounded by people in berets waxing rhapsodically about your genius. As well they should.

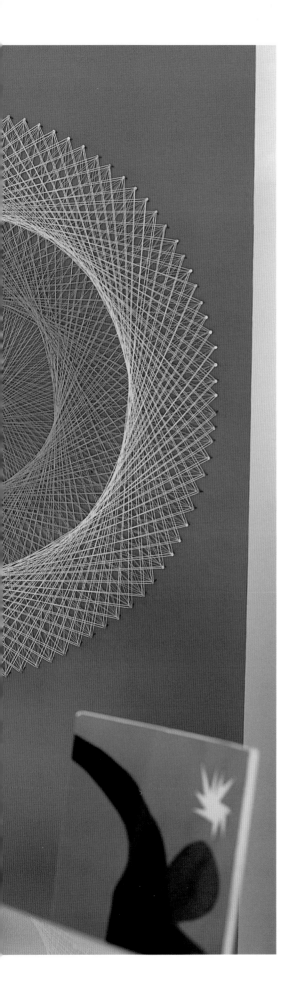

Chapter 21

Strings Attached: Creating a Wall-Sized String Art Sculpture

LEVEL OF EASE: 4

ETW (ESTIMATED TIME OF WOW): 1 hour

RECOMMENDED MUSIC: Joshua Bell. *Romance of the Violin*

If you were around in the 1970s, you may remember the string art sculptures that were so popular then. (Actually, you may not remember anything from the seventies, but we won't go there.) To jog your memory, or if you're too young to have heard of them, string art sculptures were comprised of thread going back and forth between a circle or square of nails to form a curved arc design. I loved making them in school on a little board with pins, but how would one look on a huge scale, on a wall? The answer, as you can see, is groovy.

The first thing people ask me when they see this wall is, "How long did it take you to do this?" When I tell them how easy it was to create, they can't believe it. The fact is, it is much easier to make a string art sculpture on a larger scale. Small ones can be tricky because thread is hard to maneuver around the tiny nails. But when everything is bigger, this project flies. As you weave the thread from nail to nail, it's practically therapeutic. Try it and you'll see what I mean.

Masking tape
Nails with large heads
Size 10 crochet thread in
    3 colors
String and pencil

WHERE TO BUY IT

Regular sewing thread used in standard string sculptures would be too thin and practically invisible on a wall. On the other hand, yarn would be thick enough, but it wouldn't work because it's too stretchy. The perfect solution is size 10 crochet thread, which is sold in spools of 350 yards in sewing and arts and crafts stores. It holds its shape wonderfully, comes in beautiful colors, and stands out nicely on the wall.

1 DRAW A CIRCLE ON THE WALL

To draw a circle, you'll create a makeshift compass. Gently tap a nail in the middle of the wall, where the middle of your string sculpture will be. Then tie a string around it. Extend the string to form the circle's radius and tie a pencil to the end point. Now use this compass to lightly draw a circle. Then remove the nail. Don't worry that you have a little nail hole. Either spackle it and paint over it before continuing with the project, or leave it. It will most likely be covered by the string anyway.

2 FORM A CIRCLE OF NAILS

Hammer the nails about an inch apart on the circle. If you want to be superperfect, measure every inch. When you get to the end of your circle, you might want to adjust the last few nails so they are evenly spaced. And make sure you use nails with large heads so that the string stays secure.

There is one thing you have to get over, however: nail holes. You will have a lot of them. In the sculpture pictured here, there are just over a hundred. I have a friend who lives in an apartment, and her lease says that for every nail hole she leaves when she moves, she must pay $5. If you have a landlord from Hades like this, I have one word to say to you: spackle. You can easily hide all those holes with a little spackle and paint over them.

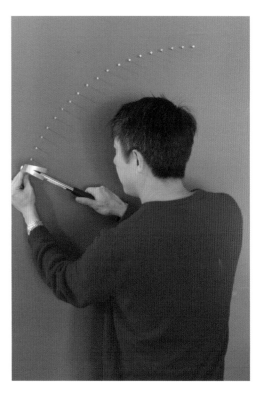

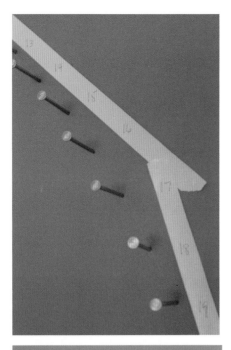

3 NUMBER THE NAILS

It is easier to thread the nails later if you number them first. Adhere some masking tape around the circumference of the circle and number each nail, #1 to whatever, in a clockwise manner.

CLOSE ENOUGH

I just estimated the space between the nails, so some of my nails were closer to each other than others. I recommend you do the same. The main consequence of this imprecision is that the circles created with the string are a little off-center. I actually like this effect because the string art looks more like an eyeball. So celebrate your lopsidedness. If everyone's string art were identical, it wouldn't be art now, would it?

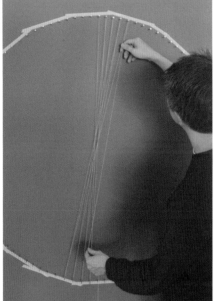

4 WEAVE THE FIRST LAYER

Now comes the therapeutic part. Take your first color and tie a knot around nail #1. Where you take the thread from here will determine the shape of this color. If you take the thread to the opposite nail, you will get a circle that is almost full. If you take the thread to a nail that's more adjacent to it, you will get a circle with a bigger hole. So let's make the first color one that's almost entirely filled up. Take the thread to the opposite side, here #51, and loop around it. Then take the thread across and loop it around nail #2, then across to nail #52, and so on.

When you have looped around the entire circle, you're not finished. Half the nails will be looped around once and half will be looped around twice. As a general rule, every nail should have two loops around it. That's what creates the pointy starbursts of the circle. Therefore, keep going another half turn until every nail has two loops around it. Then cut the thread and tie a knot around the last nail.

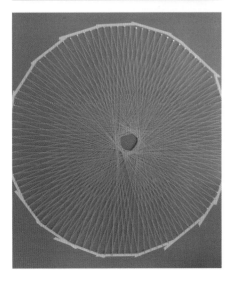

5 WEAVE THE SECOND LAYER

Next, take your second color and tie a knot around nail #1 again. For this layer, you will make a circle with a larger hole, so take the thread to a more adjacent nail, like #41. Then loop the thread around #2, then #42, #3, #43, and so on. The numbers are helpful at this point because they help you choose starting points and guide you to where the next nail is.

Again, go around the circle one-and-a-half times so that every nail has two loops around it.

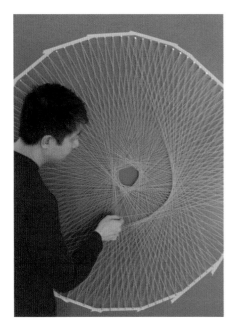

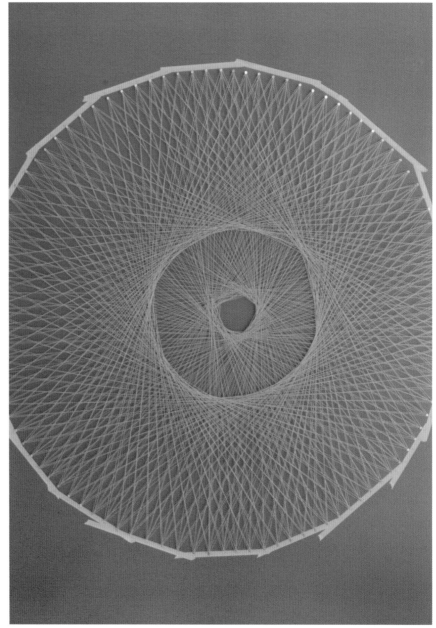

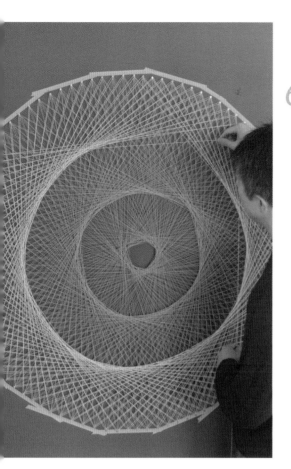

6 WEAVE THE THIRD LAYER

For the last layer, take your third color and tie a knot around nail #1. This layer will have the biggest hole, so loop the thread around #21, then #2, then #22, and so on. After you've gone around one-and-a-half times, you're done.

My instructions here produce this one pattern, but go ahead and make your own. You can create as many layers as you want, and go from large concentric circles back to small. You can even try incomplete layers so you get more of a boomerang than a circle. It's your unique stamp that makes this art.

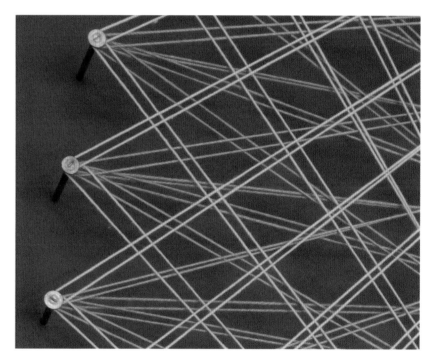

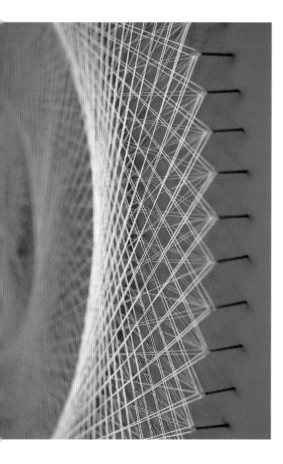

KEEPING IT CLEAN

Be very careful when cleaning your string art sculpture, because you don't want the thread to stretch or unravel. I would suggest using a compressed gas duster, which is basically air in a can. You'll find it at office supply stores, because it's used to clean computer keyboards. Just spray the clean air at the sculpture and dust flies away.

Chapter 22

It's All About You: Your Portrait Becomes a Pop Art Masterpiece

LEVEL OF EASE: 3

ETW (ESTIMATED TIME OF WOW): 3 hours

RECOMMENDED MUSIC: Madonna. *The Immaculate Collection*

Have you ever noticed that in the movies, whenever they show the home of a character who's rich and famous, there's inevitably a Warhol portrait of that character on the wall? It seems that a Warhol has become an instantly recognizable symbol of fame. So why shouldn't you have one of yourself? Your personal achievements are definitely more notable than those of a wafer-thin supermodel.

On a practical side, this Pop Art wall treatment is a colorful way to spiff up your walls without any painting or hanging artwork whatsoever. The medium is identical to that of the vinyl rub-on letters used in the wall treatment "If Walls Could Speak" (pages 96–99), and the application is also similar. But instead of words, you can make any graphic you want, including your smiling face. Now, if you're worried that people will think you're egotistical for putting huge photos of yourself on the wall, do this wall treatment with photos of a pet or a child. Or use my photo from the book jacket and plaster me all over your walls. I won't mind.

WHERE TO BUY IT

Besides the local sign shop, you can also e-mail your JPEG to a company online that will make these vinyl graphics for you. (See the Resource Directory.) They also will have a large variety of other graphics from which you can choose.

1 FIND A GOOD HEAD SHOT

First, find a good portrait of your face. Surprisingly, passport and yearbook photos work well because they're simple shots of just your head, rather than you and all your friends jammed onto a sofa. Then scan your portrait into the computer and save it as a JPEG or "psd" file. (If you don't have a scanner, go to your local copier store and they'll do it for you.)

2 POSTERIZE YOUR FACE

Next, you need to turn the scanned photograph into a black-and-white line-art graphic. Using Photoshop, go to the "Image" menu, scroll down to "Adjust," and then scroll down to "Threshold." That will immediately posterize your image into black and white. Adjust the threshold level till you get a level of posterization you like. By the way, don't scroll down to "Posterize" because that will not give you a good line-art image. Funny how that works. When you're happy, save the image as a JPEG.

Kinkos and other copier stores have computers and scanners to use (which I mention in step 1). However, they will not necessarily have a Photoshop program for you to use. If you don't have Photoshop, you can do it the low-tech way.

WHAT IF YOU DON'T HAVE PHOTOSHOP?

Before I got Photoshop, I was still able to make Pop Art portraits. Here's how I did it. Take your photograph and photocopy it. (Enlarge it, too, if necessary.) Then photocopy the photocopy. And photocopy that photocopy. Keep photocopying the copies—the more you do it, the more your face becomes posterized. You will probably have to clean up the image a bit with some correction fluid, but the results are pretty good. Then scan the image and save it as a JPEG.

3 TURN YOUR JPEG INTO VINYL GRAPHICS

Most sign shops will do this for you, so check with your local businesses. There will be a small charge to convert your JPEG into an Illustrator® file, which is the last step needed before the vinyl graphics are output. (Of course, if you have Adobe Illustrator at home, go ahead and do it yourself. It's just that most people, myself included, don't have this program.) Just tell the shop how large you want your portraits. The ones in the photos are each 24 inches wide, but you can make them any size you want, as well as any color you want.

4 ARRANGE THE GRAPHICS ON THE WALL

When you receive your vinyl graphics, tape them to the wall with masking tape at the top, lining them up with a laser level (see page 41 for instructions on how to use a laser level). You'll want to alternate colors. Also decide if you want the wall treatment to be horizontal or vertical. Feel free to constantly change your mind at this point.

5 RUB ALL LAYERS TOGETHER

As I mentioned, these graphics are made of the same vinyl material as the letters in the "If Walls Could Speak" project. Therefore, like the letters, they are also sandwiched between two layers of paper—a transfer sheet on the front and a protective sheet on the back. Burnish all the layers together with a wooden craft stick so the vinyl adheres to the top transfer sheet, as I'm doing in the photograph to the left. (*Burnish* is just a fancy word for rubbing a material with a tool.)

6 REMOVE THE BACKING SHEET

Next, carefully remove the protective backing sheet. As you're doing this, sometimes a little piece of the protective sheet tears off and sticks to the back of the vinyl. The sound of the sheet tearing is frightening, but do not be alarmed. It happens all the time. Just stop and peel off the errant piece of paper with your fingernails and continue.

7 BURNISH THE GRAPHIC

Once the protective backing sheet is removed and the transfer sheet is positioned where you want it, rub the graphic with your craft stick, paying special attention to areas where there are little details. Use the flat side of the stick to burnish large sections of the graphic at once.

HELPFUL HINT

Sometimes, after you've peeled off the protective sheet, the entire piece comes off the wall, masking tape and all. Oh no! Actually, it's no biggie. Just reapply the piece on the wall. At this point, you can reapply and remove the piece frequently. The transfer paper is sticky, so it holds onto the wall really easily; and as long as you don't press onto the vinyl yet, you can keep repositioning the sheet.

8 PEEL OFF THE TRANSFER LAYER

Here is where the application of these graphics differs from that of the vinyl letters. Letters are relatively skinny and small, so removing the transfer layer is rather easy. However, when you peel off the transfer sheet of these graphics, you have to be more careful because the image is larger. Work very slowly. When you're removing the top sheet, the graphic will often bubble on the wall because it hasn't been burnished enough. But it's easy to remedy. Just use the flat edge of the wooden stick and rub directly on the exposed vinyl graphic, smoothing it onto the wall. Keep lifting a little of the transfer sheet at a time and smooth out the exposed vinyl. If you get a few creases here and there, so what. As you can see below, you get a colorful and dramatic look when you're finished. This wall will definitely be famous for more than fifteen minutes.

KEEPING IT CLEAN

In most situations, a damp cloth will do just fine. If someone's drawn a mustache on your face, you don't need a cleaner, you need new friends.

REMOVING THE ARTWORK

When you want to remove the artwork, peel it off slowly and carefully. Because so much of the graphic has adhered to the wall, you want to avoid lifting paint off with it. The trick is to heat the vinyl with a blow dryer and peel it off at a 90-degree angle as the dryer does its magic. This is how they remove decals from cars without damaging the paint.

Chapter 23

Noteworthy: An Eye-Popping Kaleidoscope of Post-it® Notes

LEVEL OF EASE: (2)

ETW (ESTIMATED TIME OF WOW): 5 hours

RECOMMENDED MUSIC: Cindi Lauper. *True Colors*

When I told people that I was going to design a wall treatment made of Post-it® Notes, they thought I was crazy. While I may have my moments of lunacy, I was quite lucid when I imagined a wall covered with these square, self-adhesive note papers of different colors. I'm happy to say that after seeing this wall in person, all the naysayers couldn't believe how striking the effect was. Straight on, the Post-it Notes look like mosaic tiles, while from the side they look like psychedelic roof shingles.

I originally meant for this wall design to be included in either the "Pulp Power" or "Ideas that Stick" sections of the book. But after completing it, the wall looked like a contemporary art installation, so I've placed it here. You can say it's a witty piece that satirizes corporate operations and office systems.

WHERE TO BUY IT

As tempting as it may be, don't go to the supply cabinet of the company you work for to steal Post-it Notes. Besides, they probably won't have the Super Sticky variety. Go to your local office supply store, and you'll find these Post-it Notes in an assortment of colors. One pack usually has around 450 individual sheets, so you only need to buy two packs.

1 START AT THE BOTTOM OF THE WALL

Shine a laser level horizontally about 2 feet from the bottom of the wall. You don't want the Post-it Notes going any farther down than this because working so low to the ground is very difficult on the back and knees. Besides, you don't need to go floor to ceiling to create an awesome effect.

Line up the top of your first Post-it Note with the laser level line and press it onto the wall. You may be asking if the adhesive on the Post-it Notes is enough to keep them secure. Good question. The regular Post-it Notes aren't sticky enough. That's why you should buy the Super Sticky ones. They'll stay up as long as you want. I even flung my body against the wall of Post-it Notes to see if they'd stay on and only a handful fell off. Then one stuck to the back of my shirt and stayed there all day without my knowing it.

2 COMPLETE THE FIRST HORIZONTAL ROW

Keep lining the Post-it Notes, one after the other, with the laser level line. You can alternate colors, but it's also fine to repeat colors now and then. You want the look to be random. In this wall treatment, I've chosen four different colors, and I don't recommend any more. At first, I used a fifth color, and that one extra color was enough to make my eyes hurt.

3 START THE NEXT ROW

Now move the laser level up so that when you line up the next row of Post-it Notes, the top Post-it overlaps the one below by about a half-inch. This creates the "shingle" effect. Also, you'll notice that many of the Post-its will fan out naturally from the wall. By overlapping them slightly, you see the Post-it Notes underneath, rather than the wall itself, when they fan out.

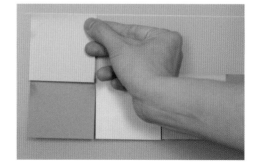

4 KEEP GOING

Go ahead and continue this second row, lining up the top of each Post-it Note to the laser level line. I'm having you start at the bottom and work to the top of the wall, which makes it easier for you to overlap the top Post-its over the bottom ones. Overall, this wall treatment is super easy to complete. The only reason I've rated it a 2 instead of 1 for "level of ease" is that the repetitive nature of sticking the notes to the wall is hard on the shoulders. Take lots of lemonade breaks.

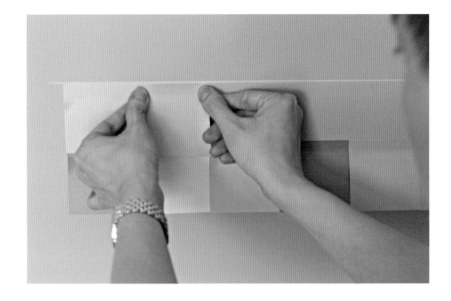

5 PRESS DOWN ON THE POST-IT NOTES AGAIN

Periodically press down at the top of the Post-it Notes where the adhesive is to make sure they're secure to the wall. As I said, they may flair out from the wall, and that's great. We just want the top of the Post-it Notes to stick.

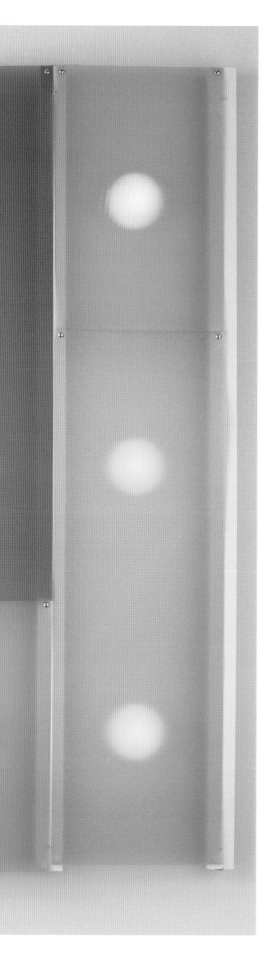

Chapter 24

Razzle Dazzle: Tap the Lights and Turn on the Color

> **LEVEL OF EASE:** ⑤
>
> **ETW (ESTIMATED TIME OF WOW):** 8 hours
>
> **RECOMMENDED MUSIC:** 1996 Broadway Revival Cast.
> *Chicago—The Musical*

Now that you're all experts in creating stylish wall treatments, I've saved the *piece de resistance* for last. It's an interactive showpiece of multicolored plastic sheets forming a Mondrian-like pattern. On their own, they already look splendid. But hidden behind them are lights, which turn on when you touch them so that the wall glows with color.

The inspiration for this interactive showpiece came from two unlikely sources. First was the late-night commercials for touch lights, those moon-shaped battery-operated lights that light up when you tap on them. They're usually used in closets and bathrooms. The second source of inspiration was a selection of plastic binder covers my friend Sandi had borrowed from a printer. I saw the ribbed plastic in a variety of bright colors and thought they would look great on a wall. So I married the two ideas together for one spectacular wall treatment.

Although I must admit that I struggled a bit with the installation of this piece, the individual steps really aren't that difficult. It's just that I am the least handy person in the world. I do not have the carpenter gene. I tell you this because if I can do it, anybody can. And after this wall was completed, every difficulty was quickly forgotten because the result was so fantastic. (Kind of like childbirth, or so I'm told.)

1 NAIL THE TWO TYPES OF BOARDS TOGETHER

First, we need to build the frame that the plastic sheets will be screwed onto. It has to have a little depth so that the touch lights can sit in it. This step is the "carpenter" portion of the installation, and the one I had the most difficulty with. But if you or someone you know is good with a power screwdriver, you're already ahead of me.

I chose to use medium-density fiberboard (MDF) and redwood boards that are 6 feet long because they: a) are precut in those lengths; b) fit perfectly within an 8-foot-high wall; and c) fit in my car. (Instead of redwood boards, you can also use Douglas fir or any other prefinished wood boards available at the lumberyard or home improvement warehouse.) The redwood board is narrower than the MDF. Place a 2-x-2 redwood board on top of the 1-x-3 MDF and hammer the two strips together with two nails, one at the top and one at the bottom. Select nails that are more than 2 inches long but less than 3 inches long so they don't go through the other side. Also, nail on the redwood board side because it's the MDF side that will be facing out.

Why do we have to nail these two boards together? Basically, we need a frame with a depth of about 3 inches, because that is the depth of the touch lights. One board alone would not be deep enough. We're placing the wider board on the outside, so it appears to float on top of the 2-x-2. Repeat this procedure so you have seven beams altogether.

WHERE TO BUY IT

I tracked down the manufacturer of the ribbed polypropylene, PVC Tech. They usually sell only to wholesale manufacturers, as this plastic is used for things like binder covers. So I asked if they would sell to a normal consumer like me, and they said they were not only happy to sell to consumers, they were thrilled that people were finding new uses for their plastic. So give them a call. They will ship anywhere in the country, too. There is a minimum order, but it's small. As for the lumber in this project, go to a home improvement warehouse for the best selection. While you're there, you'll also find plenty of touch lights.

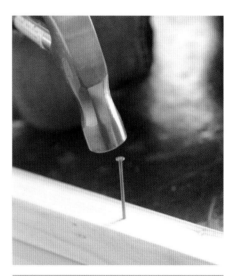

2 SCREW THE FIRST BEAM INTO THE WALL

Next, drill two centered holes through both boards, one at the top and one at the bottom. Make sure they're at the same relative location on all seven beams. These holes are for the screws that will affix the beams to the wall. Use screws that are longer than 3 inches. If you're screwing into plain drywall, you will want to screw into drywall anchors.

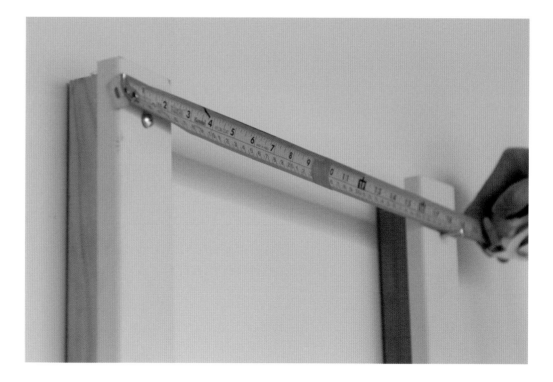

3 SCREW A BEAM INTO THE WALL EVERY 16 INCHES

The second beam should be parallel to the first, with the inside edges of the beams 16 inches apart. In fact, all subsequent beams should be 16 inches apart. You'll see why I insist on this distance later.

The MDF is preprimed, so you can paint it after it's screwed on the wall. I painted the boards white, and painted over the screws so they would disappear. What you will have is seven beams screwed on the wall, creating six vertical rows in which to place the plastic sheets and touch lights.

4 INSTALL THE LIGHTS

Space the touch lights evenly, three lights per row, within the beams. Use a small nail to hang each of them. Try to get all the lights lined up straight horizontally and vertically. Of course, insert batteries into the lights before installing them.

5 CUT THE PLASTIC

The ribbed polypropylene comes in a standard size of 24 x 48 inches. The width of 24 inches is more than you need. Cut the sheets to a width of 18 inches. It's really easy to cut using an X-Acto knife, and the ribbed lines give you a guide to cut lengthwise. After cutting them into 18-x-48-inch sheets, cut some of them in half, to 18 x 24 inches. This way, each vertical row will have one panel that's 18-x-48 inches and one that's 18 x 24 inches, for a total size of 18 x 72 inches (6 feet—just like the length of the beams!).

6 SCREW IN THE PLASTIC SHEETS

Start with the longer 48-inch piece of plastic. It is 18 inches wide, while the space between the beams is 16 inches wide. Therefore, there is 1 inch on either side of the plastic that will lie on top of the beam. Using a small, flat-headed screw, attach the plastic on the left beam and the right beam. To make it easier, you may first want to drill a small hole in the plastic and wood where you want to attach it to the beam. And remember to use a drill bit that's one size smaller than the screw, so the screw fits snuggly.

Since you've started with the 48-inch piece of plastic, you will finish the row with the shorter 24-inch piece. For the next row, you will alternate.

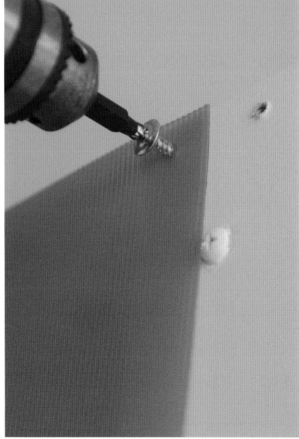

7 ADHERE THE BOTTOMS WITH VELCRO

Instead of screwing the bottoms of each plastic sheet onto the beams, attach them with small Velcro dots. That will make it easier to lift the plastic when you want to change the batteries of the touch lights.

I hope you've seen that the steps to install this wall treatment are by themselves pretty simple. It just helps to have the basic ability to use a hammer, drill, and screwdriver. I wasn't so good with them before I started, but now I feel like an old pro. Or at least an experienced novice.

KEEPING IT CLEAN

For the exterior plastic, some household cleaner and a towel will do the trick. Inside, especially around the wood beams, the hose attachment of a vacuum cleaner will work best to remove any dust.

SUIT YOUR MOOD

You don't have to turn on all the lights at the same time. Sometimes you may be in a blue mood, or an orange mood, so just tap on the lights under those colors. Even just one light on can make an impact. It's totally up to you.

Acknowledgments

Somebody pinch me. As I put the finishing touches on this book, I still can't believe it, and not just because I always thought my first book would be a trashy novel. My life has been blessed with people who've opened doors for me and taken me in new directions I never dreamed possible. I wouldn't be here without them.

First of all, I want to thank the extraordinary team at Watson-Guptill, starting with Victoria Craven. Gifts and flowers will never be enough to repay her for her vision and support, so if I ever have children, she gets dibs on the firstborn. My editor, Holly Jennings, was an author's dream, with her keen eye, thoughtful insights, and sunny personality. Production manager Ellen Greene took piles of disparate elements and made magic out of them. And Areta Buk and Pooja Bakri took my breath away with cover and layout designs that absolutely captured the spirit of the book.

Many thanks to the classiest agent in the world, Deborah Warren. She is my literary soul mate. My book coach, Monique Raphel High, for her wisdom and guidance. Bill Stark, my publicist, who's more excited about this book than anyone. Media coach Jacquie Jordan, for reminding me to smile. Everyone who let me disrupt their lives so I could photograph their wall treatments: Megan Geckler, Carol Lee, Sara Sweedler, Tova, Shanni and David Suissa, Kim Harrington, Angie Horejsi, Lori and Jake Indgin, and Matt D'Amico and Christina Kogos at 10th Street Entertainment. My friends and colleagues Margaret Mendenhall, Karyn Anderson, Sandy Weinstock, Taryn Wayne, Anita Levine, Troy Thompsen, Monica Heeren, Ellen Allan, and Laurie Faulkner, who gave me technical advice, lugged furniture and supplies, and held the ladder for me. Bobi Leonard, for affirmations of success that still ring in my ear. David Zyla, who introduced me to the wonderful world of color. Jessica Boone, my uber-talented photographer and partner in crime. And the dear people who started me on this adventure: Noel Evans, Drew Hallmann, and Maryann Welker. If I had an applause machine, I'd turn it on for you all.

Special thanks to the one-and-only Kitty Bartholomew, who took me under her wing and encouraged me to fly. I am forever grateful.

I also want to thank the thousands of people from around the globe who visit my Web site, jonathanfongstyle.com, every day. I am humbled by their loyalty and enthusiasm. They are my inspiration.

Thanks to Oprah Winfrey, who will have me on her show one day.

And finally, thanks to Greg Phillips, for making the best chocolate chip cookies in the world.

Resource Directory

All of the materials used for the wall treatments in this book are readily available. I can't carry much in the back of my Mini Cooper, so I shopped a lot on the Internet and had items shipped to me. Therefore, you can easily access these online sources regardless of where you live. For items I bought from local merchants, you can contact them directly or find comparable stores near you.

Aluminum Roof Flashing, Copper Tube Caps, Copper Wire Straps, Hardware Cloth, Medium-Density Fiberboard, Redwood Boards, Touch Lights, Wood Stain and Sealer
So many of the projects in this book start at your local home improvement warehouse. I feel like I spend more time in these stores than at furniture stores.
The following stores are located throughout the U.S.
The Home Depot
www.homedepot.com
Lowes
www.lowes.com

Balsa Wood Sheets
It's so hard to find balsa wood sheets that are wider than 6 inches. I've only come across one Web site that sells 12-inch-wide sheets, and they have them in different lengths and thicknesses.
National Balsa Co.
(413) 596-2507
www.nationalbalsa.com
The following Web site offers 8-inch-wide sheets, which will give you narrower panels; but they work just as well.
Specialized Balsa Wood, LLC
(970) 461-WOOD
www.specializedbalsa.com

Bamboo Spray Branches
Look for bamboo as well as other dried branches at your local craft store.
Moskatel's
733 S. San Julian
Los Angeles, CA 90014
(213) 689-4830
Jo-Ann Fabrics and Crafts
Locations throughout the U.S.
www.joann.com

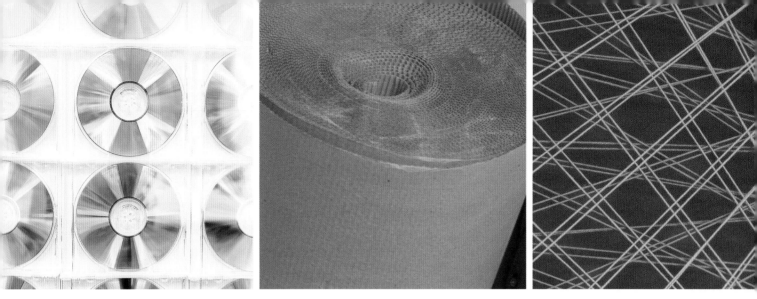

Canvas

For canvas, look for art supply stores that cater to painters. They'll have the big rolls, all primed and ready to go.
Pearl Art & Craft Supply
Many locations in ten states
www.pearlpaint.com
Other online stores:
www.allenscanvas.com
www.americanhomeandhabitat.com
www.dickblick.com
www.textilesforyou.com

Compact Discs and Jewel Cases

You won't have any trouble finding CDs and jewel cases, at least until technology takes another giant leap.
The following stores are located throughout the U.S.
Office Depot
www.officedepot.com
Staples
www.staples.com
Target
www.target.com
Best Buy
www.bestbuy.com
Other online stores:
www.uline.com
www.sleevetown.com
www.musiciansfriend.com
www.shop4tech.com

Corrugated Cardboard

Your local shipping and packing store can order you the b-flute corrugated rolls needed for the wall treatment in Chapter 11, or you can do as I did and order the rolls online.
www.papermart.com
www.brasspack.com
The following Web site carries the corrugated rolls in white, for a completely different look.
www.packagingsupplies.com

Crochet Thread

I had never shopped for thread or yarn before, so I didn't realize what a booming business it is. If your city hasn't caught on to the "homespun" craze, here are a few places where I found crochet thread.
Joann Fabrics and Crafts
Locations throughout the U.S.
www.joann.com
And at these online stores:
www.herrschners.com
www.artscraftsstore.com
www.knitting-warehouse.com

Fabric

The following Web sites are good sources for fabrics, but there's nothing like going to a fabric store, so you can see and touch the different varieties in person.
www.hancockfabrics.com
www.denverfabrics.com
www.fashionfabricsclub.com

Foam Core

You can find foam core at almost any arts and crafts store in your neighborhood, as well as at the following online retailers.
The Art Store/Dick Blick Art Materials
Many locations in sixteen states
www.dickblick.com
Other online suppliers:
www.cheapjoes.com
www.artsupply.com
www.masterg.com

Magnetic Paint

I looked all over for magnetic paint, and my local paint stores had a very limited supply, if any. So do as I did—go to the source.
Kling Magnetics
343 Rt. 295
P.O. Box 348
Chatham, NY 12037
(518) 392-4000
www.kling.com

Magnetic Tape

If your local craft or office supply store doesn't carry magnetic tape, here are some online sources. This self-adhesive tape is fun to have on hand, as it will turn anything into a magnet.
www.shoplet.com
www.magnetsource.com
www.discountofficesupplies.com

Mod Podge

While you can find Mod Podge at most arts and crafts stores, I like the big gallon size, which is more readily available online.
www.dickblick.com
www.plaidonline.com
www.save-on-crafts.com
www.createforless.com

Paper Doilies

As I said already, paper doilies are everywhere. I bought mine at Bed, Bath & Beyond, but they're probably right under your nose (and your chocolate éclair).
Bed, Bath & Beyond
Locations throughout the U.S.
www.bedbathandbeyond.com
And at:
www.surlatable.com

Paper Tape

The Permacel paper tape (official name: Colored Printable Kraft Paper, #P724) I've used in this book is available in some art supply stores, but for a complete assortment of colors, check the following stores and Web sites.
Studio Depot
900 N. La Brea Ave.
Hollywood, CA 90038
(323) 851-0111
www.studiodepot.com
Filmtools
3100 W. Magnolia Blvd.
Burbank, CA 91505
(888) 807-1900
www.filmtools.com

Polypropylene Sheets

For ribbed polypropylene sheets, give this company a call, and they'll be glad to help you. Look on their Web site for available colors (scroll horizontally to about the middle of the page).
PVC Tech Corp.
1931 E. Vista Bella Way
Dominguez Hills, CA 90220
(310) 608-1115
www.pvctech.com/pages/pg_polypro/
pp_sheet.shtml

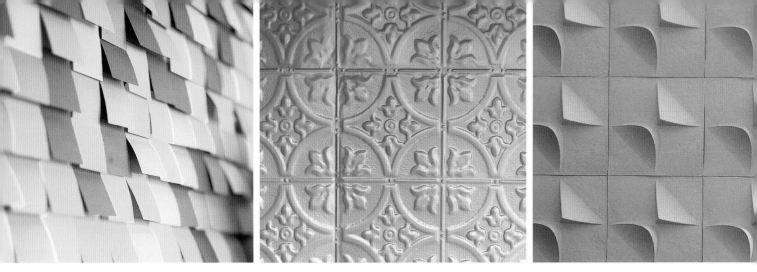

Post-it Notes

Of course, you can find Post-it Notes everywhere. Just remember to look for the Super Sticky ones. The following stores are located throughout the U.S.

www.staples.com
www.officedepot.com
www.officemax.com

Test Tubes

Many educational supply retailers carry test tubes, but they are usually made of plastic. You can buy the glass ones, made by Klimax® or Pyrex™, at the following online stores.

www.sciencecompany.com
www.scienceprojects.net

Tin Ceiling Panels

These are just a couple of the manufacturers of tin ceiling panels. The customer service people are very helpful if you tell them what you're planning to do.

The American Tin Ceiling Co.
1800 Northgate Blvd., Suite A-6
Sarasota, FL 34234
(888) 231-7500
www.americantinceilings.com
M-Boss, Inc.
5350 Grant Ave.
Cleveland, OH 44125
(866) 886-2677
www.mbossinc.com

V2 Wallpaper Tiles

Those fantastic V2 tiles are available direct from the manufacturer.

Mio
340 N. 12th St., Unit 301
Philadelphia, PA 19107
(215) 925-9359
www.mioculture.com

Vinyl Wall Letters, Vinyl Graphics

My local sign shop introduced me to the endless possibilities of vinyl letters and graphics. Check with your neighborhood store, or look for the online stores below.

Santa Monica Signs, Inc.
1806 Lincoln Blvd.
Santa Monica, CA 90404
(310) 399-3067
www.geometryhome.com
www.wallwords.com
www.wallphrases.com
www.wisedecor.com

Other Resources

Furniture and accessories featured in Chapters 6, 7, 8, 10, 12, 17, 18, and 24.
Loft Appeal
903 S. Hill St.
Los Angeles, CA 90015
(213) 629-9105

Original paintings featured in Chapters 17 and 18.
Douglas C. Bloom
www.douglascbloom.com

INDEX

" The best rooms don't reflect
who you are, **but who you want to be.**"